Presidential Assassins

Other Books in the History Makers Series:

*History*MAKERS

Presidential Assassins

By Patricia D. Netzley

Lucent Books
P.O. Box 289011, San Diego, CA 92198-9011

Library of Congress Cataloging-in-Publication Data

Netzley, Patricia D.
    Presidential assassins / by Patricia D. Netzley.
        p.   cm. — (History makers)
    Includes bibliographical references (p.) and index.
    Summary: Traces the lives and motives of American assassins or
would-be assassins and their impact on history.
    ISBN 1-56006-623-7 (lib. : alk. paper)
    1. Assassins—United States—Biography—Juvenile literature. 2.
Presidents—United States—Assassination—History—Juvenile literature.
(U.S.) Biography—Juvenile literature.   3. Presidents—United States—
Assassination attempts—History—Juvenile literature. [1. Assassins. 2.
Presidents—Assassination. 3. Presidents—Assassination attempts.]
I. Title.   II. Series
E176.1 .N45 2000
364.15'2'0922—dc21   99-049396

Cover photos: Lynette Alice "Squeaky" Fromme (center), Lee Harvey
Oswald (top right), Leon Czolgosz (botom right), John Wilkes Booth
(lower left), Charles Guiteau (top left)

Copyright 2000 by Lucent Books, Inc.
P.O. Box 289011, San Diego, California 92198-9011

Printed in the U.S.A.

CONTENTS

FOREWORD

The literary form most often referred to as "multiple biography" was perfected in the first century A.D. by Plutarch, a perceptive and talented moralist and historian who hailed from the small town of Chaeronea in central Greece. His most famous work, *Parallel Lives*, consists of a long series of biographies of noteworthy ancient Greek and Roman statesmen and military leaders. Frequently, Plutarch compares a famous Greek to a famous Roman, pointing out similarities in personality and achievements. These expertly constructed and very readable tracts provided later historians and others, including playwrights like Shakespeare, with priceless information about prominent ancient personages and also inspired new generations of writers to tackle the multiple biography genre.

The Lucent History Makers series proudly carries on the venerable tradition handed down from Plutarch. Each volume in the series consists of a set of five to eight biographies of important and influential historical figures who were linked together by a common factor. In *Rulers of Ancient Rome*, for example, all the figures were generals, consuls, or emperors of either the Roman Republic or Empire; while the subjects of *Fighters Against American Slavery*, though they lived in different places and times, all shared the same goal, namely the eradication of human servitude. Mindful that politicians and military leaders are not (and never have been) the only people who shape the course of history, the editors of the series have also included representatives from a wide range of endeavors, including scientists, artists, writers, philosophers, religious leaders, and sports figures.

Each book is intended to give a range of figures—some well known, others less known; some who made a great impact on history, others who made only a small impact. For instance, by making Columbus's initial voyage possible, Spain's Queen Isabella I, featured in *Women Leaders of Nations*, helped to open up the New World to exploration and exploitation by the European powers. Unarguably, therefore, she made a major contribution to a series of events that had momentous consequences for the entire world. By contrast, Catherine II, the eighteenth-century Russian queen, and Golda Meir, the modern Israeli prime minister, did not play roles of global impact; however, their policies and actions significantly influenced the historical development of both their own countries and their regional neighbors. Regardless of their relative importance in the greater historical scheme, all of the figures chronicled in the History Makers series made contributions to posterity; and their public achievements, as well as what is known about their private lives, are presented and evaluated in light of the most recent scholarship.

In addition, each volume in the series is documented and substantiated by a wide array of primary and secondary source quotations. The primary source quotes enliven the text by presenting eyewitness views of the times and culture in which each history maker lived; while the secondary source quotes, taken from the works of respected modern scholars, offer expert elaboration and/ or critical commentary. Each quote is footnoted, demonstrating to the reader exactly where biographers find their information. The footnotes also provide the reader with the means of conducting additional research. Finally, to further guide and illuminate readers, each volume in the series features photographs, two bibliographies, and a comprehensive index.

The History Makers series provides both students engaged in research and more casual readers with informative, enlightening, and entertaining overviews of individuals from a variety of circumstances, professions, and backgrounds. No doubt all of them, whether loved or hated, benevolent or cruel, constructive or destructive, will remain endlessly fascinating to each new generation seeking to identify the forces that shaped their world.

A Unique Type of Murder

Four American presidents have been killed by assassins: Abraham Lincoln by John Wilkes Booth; James Garfield by Charles Guiteau; William McKinley by Leon Czolgosz; and John F. Kennedy by Lee Harvey Oswald (although Oswald's guilt remains a matter of controversy). Each assassination brought changes in laws and public policy, and each affected the way that the American people viewed the presidency and the country.

Almost every American president has experienced an assassination attempt, most notably Andrew Jackson, Theodore Roosevelt, Franklin Roosevelt, Harry Truman, Gerald Ford, and Ronald Reagan. Some of these attempts were more jolting to the national consciousness than others. For example, the attempt to kill Ronald Reagan deeply upset the American public because it came very close to succeeding.

The assassination attempt on Gerald Ford by Lynette "Squeaky" Fromme upset the public as well. In addition, Fromme's act inspired other assassins to attempt the same deed. In his autobiography *A Time to Heal,* Ford recounts that he was receiving about a hundred written threats a month at the time of Fromme's attack, and shortly thereafter he was shot at by Sara Jane Moore, who had ties to radical groups. Both Fromme and Moore insisted that their act was politically motivated, but Ford considered them mentally ill. He specifically referred to Fromme

Theodore Roosevelt is one of many presidents who have been the targets of assassination attempts.

as one of the "misfits and kooks [that have appeared] in every society since the beginning of time."[1]

Many experts in criminal behavior believe that all American presidential assassins suffer from some form of mental illness. In fact, criminologist Jack Levin of Boston argues that this is the major difference between American assassins and those elsewhere in the world. He reports that foreign assassinations are far more likely to involve terrorist groups that are killing a leader because of a political cause, adding, "In Europe and the Middle East, the dangers . . . are political. Ours [are] from psychotics."[2]

In fact, the Secret Service, which is charged with protecting the president, says that thousands of mentally ill people have made oral or written threats against the nation's chief executive. But when a mentally ill person goes one step further and actually shoots the leader of the world's most powerful nation, the event takes on far greater significance than any other crime. The death of a U.S. president can change the course of history, both in America and the world.

CHAPTER 1

Political and Personal Causes

U.S. presidents have always been vulnerable to assassination, in part because the nature of American politics requires them to remain accessible to the public despite the risks involved with face-to-face contact. History offers many accounts of people who have tried to kill American presidents, and these assassination attempts differ noticeably from those in countries where leaders are more difficult to reach. Scholar James McKinley summarizes the unique qualities of American assassination:

> Assassination has been with the world almost forever, and Americans came to it relatively late. We also came to it differently. Before ours, for a time nearly out of mind, assassins had been those who calmly killed a public figure out of a clear political motivation. . . . [The typical] Old World assassin . . . [was] cool, relentless, often organized into terrorist teams, and perfectly willing to die for the cause.

> But American assassins broke this pattern. They have not, it seems, habitually banded together for their task, just as they haven't much gone in for slaying low-level officials, a frequent phenomenon in other countries. They are attracted instead to the President or to similarly striking figures. . . . Cases of conspiracy—so prevalent elsewhere in the world—are difficult to prove in most American assassinations.[3]

Mental Illness

Perhaps the most striking feature of those who attempt to assassinate the president is their history of mental instability. The first person to make an attempt on the life of an American president was Richard Lawrence, a housepainter who tried to shoot President Andrew Jackson on January 30, 1835. Lawrence was clearly insane; he believed himself to be King Richard III of England and Jackson to be the king who had usurped his throne. Other presidential assassins have also exhibited signs of mental illness, even those claiming to have committed their act as part of a political cause. For this reason, Albert Ellis and John M. Gullo, who have studied assassins in depth, believe that, regardless of their motivation, all American assassins are likely to be insane:

Richard Lawrence, who attempted to assassinate President Andrew Jackson (pictured), believed he was King Richard III of England.

> Although on the surface, assassination may seem to be a cold-blooded result of political partisanship, it is our contention that it rarely is. [C]ontemporary assassins . . . almost always prove to be exceptionally deranged individuals. Some of them, in fact, appear to have few or no political motives. . . .
>
> We may even suspect that most members of revolutionary groups . . . who openly advocate and sometimes dramatically carry out "political" assassinations, adhere to their creeds of violence not merely because of their social ideologies but because they *want* to kill. They may *say* that they are would-be or actual assassins because they passionately want to fight against oppression and that they have dispassionately figured out that political murder is an effective method of upholding the ideologies in which they believe; but we have to suspect that they are also driven to their deeds by less altruistic motives.[4]

Ellis and Gullo conclude that,

> with few exceptions, public assassins of outstanding political figures tend to be psychotic. They generally have long histories of emotionally aberrated behavior; they often suffer specific life crises just before they kill; and they murder in a senseless manner as far as their political beliefs and aspirations are concerned.[5]

The Assassin Personality

But aside from mental illness, presidential assassins share certain personality traits. In fact, they have so much in common that psychologists have been able to develop an "assassin profile." This profile identifies behaviors that assassins typically exhibit in their lives prior to committing their crime, information that might one day be used to prevent an assassination. In summarizing the assassin profile, former FBI agent and assassination expert John Douglas says,

> Regardless of the specifics of the crime, regardless of the so-called cause, the violent act is the result of a deep-seated feeling of inadequacy on the part of the assassin. . . . No matter who we look at, we're going to find an individual—overwhelmingly, a white male in his twenties—who does

Would-be assassin Sara Jane Moore leaves court. Psychologists claim that assassins share certain personality traits that can be used to form "assassin profiles."

not feel good about himself and never has. In some way, he sees the violent act as the solution to his problem.[6]

Ellis and Gullo agree that the typical assassin feels inferior to other people. They report on a study of the assassin personality in which scholar L. S. Clemens found that assassins were "failures—in work, in play, and in life" and that "their dismal failures in life, and their consequent feelings of inadequacy, were important factors in driving them to do away with powerful presidential figures who obviously were just as successful as they were not."[7] Similarly, Douglas says that the typical assassin thinks, "I'm not as worthy as anyone else. I'm just an inadequate nobody, and the only way I can become important is by some great act that affects all those important people."[8]

By killing a president, an assassin has the chance to become a "somebody" instead of a "nobody"; every assassin, successful or not, has changed history in some way. As James McKinley reports,

> Assassination ordains the death of a leader. Assassination changes things. The people who govern us change, and our laws change, and our policies shift, and the governmental system is re-examined, even modified. But most of all, the assassination—so sudden, so unexpected, so terrible—shocks us into new consciousness, and *we* are fundamentally changed.[9]

The assassin's target is not only a person but also an entire country. Douglas explains: "The president of the United States . . . represents the nation—all that's good and bad about it—in the assassin's mind."[10] A presidential assassination, therefore, is an act of anger against a system that has likely offered the assassin little reward.

However, the assassins themselves typically deny that they are acting out of anger or insanity. Instead, assassins usually say that their act has been committed for the good of the American people. They have a rigid view of what is right for the country and dismiss anyone who does not agree with them. As Ellis and Gullo report,

> The typical political assassin . . . dogmatically and authoritarianly . . . *demands* that his own views be considered absolutely right and everyone else's utterly fallacious; *insists* on making himself the final arbiter of human destiny, while placing all those who dissent from his views on an infinitely lower, dehumanized, and preferably nonexistent level.[11]

As a result, assassins perceive themselves as heroes. For example, Ellis and Gullo quote another researcher of the assassin personality, Robert J. Donovan, as saying,

> None of the assassins [studied, including Richard Lawrence, Charles Guiteau, Leon Czolgosz, and would-be assassin Guiseppe Zangara] repented his deed. To a man

Guiseppe Zangara reads about his assassination attempt. Assassins usually do not feel any remorse for their actions.

they felt their acts had been justified. Zangara went so far as to say that his only regret was that he had failed to kill Franklin Roosevelt. Others maintained they had done their duty. Some considered themselves martyrs.[12]

One way that American assassins may differ from their counterparts elsewhere is their expectation of how their act will be perceived by other Americans. McKinley suggests that the disparity between how assassins think they will be judged and how they are actually judged is due to their faulty mental processes:

> Perhaps the unique characteristic of the *American* assassination is that the assassin misunderstands the nation in whose cause he thinks he kills. *He is a poor historian, though he believes otherwise.* In his linear and insular reasoning, things must proceed as fantasized in his own delusions.[13]

Out of Touch with Society

In other words, the assassin incorrectly assesses presidential policies and public opinion. For example, John Wilkes Booth assumed that Abraham Lincoln's vice president, Andrew Johnson, would treat the South better after the Civil War than Lincoln would; therefore, Booth thought he was helping the South by killing the president. In fact, Johnson's views on how the South should be treated were far harsher than Lincoln's had been. Similarly, Leon Czolgosz thought that William McKinley's death would promote his anarchist views, but after the assassination, the public rejected anarchism and persecuted anarchists. Lee Harvey Oswald believed that John F. Kennedy's death would bring him acclaim in the Soviet Union, but the Russians disavowed any involvement in his act and called him insane.

Would-be assassins suffer from the same flaws in reasoning. For example, Lynette "Squeaky" Fromme believed that her attempt on President Gerald Ford's life would bring attention to environmental issues as well as to injustices she believed had been carried out in the murder trial of her mentor, Charles Manson. However, public awareness and concern about these issues remained unchanged. John W. Hinckley Jr. was certain that his assassination attempt would make him popular; in reality, however, he was vilified for his deed.

Whatever the state of their mental health, it is the nature of assassins to misunderstand society. This is partly because assassins

John Hinckley Jr. believed that he would become a hero if he assassinated President Reagan.

typically have grown up as outcasts. For this reason, few American assassins have even tried to commit their act as part of a conspiracy. The assassin personality does not lend itself to the cooperation and trust usually required to work as part of a team.

Moreover, American assassins are typically impatient, which also makes it difficult for them to plan their acts carefully, as most conspiracies require. Ellis and Gullo believe that this impatience is part of the flawed thinking that is so common among assassins:

Political assassins . . . usually are individuals with low frustration tolerance and lack of prolonged discipline, who want—or rather, demand—what they want when they want it. Which means: immediately, pronto, *right now!* . . . However worthy their causes may be (or may seem to be in their own biased eyes), assassins are frequently unwilling to keep *working* to achieve the goals they seek; and they impatiently, and to a large extent mystically, believe that they will be able to attain them at one fell, dramatic swoop. Sudden assassination of their foes is therefore their frequent (and usually quite unrealistic) choice.[14]

But assassins crave more than results; they also crave the spotlight of public attention. As Ellis and Gullo point out, assassination is typically a public act not only because the president is more accessible when out in public but also because assassins crave fame. Ellis and Gullo report that

the assassin frequently commits his act of murder publicly, in full view of hundreds or even thousands of people. This is partly because he would have great difficulty in achieving a private interview with the man he is determined to kill. But it is also partly because he *wants* to be seen doing this thing and is rather proud of the fact that he does it in front of witnesses.[15]

Protecting the President

Although experts know many details about the assassin personality, they cannot use this information to prevent assassinations. Most people who fit the assassin profile do not follow through on their desire to kill the president, and it would be unjust to arrest someone merely for a personality trait or a violent thought. However, certain things can be done to minimize the risk of presidential assassination. For example, James McKinley says, "political campaigns could be conducted more via the media and less by pressing the flesh [shaking hands]."[16]

But President Ford argues against this, believing that it is important for the president to remain undaunted by assassination attempts:

> I don't think any person as President ought to cower in the face of a limited number of people who want to take the law into their own hands. The American people want a dialogue between them and their President and their other public officials. And if we can't have that opportunity of talking with one another, seeing one another, shaking hands with one another, something has gone wrong in our society. I think it's important that we as a people don't capitulate to the wrong element, an infinitesimal number of

Richard Nixon acknowledges a group of his supporters. Some people think that it is dangerous for a president to be so available to the public.

people who want to destroy everything that's best about America.[17]

McKinley, too, acknowledges that isolating the president would be a detriment to a democracy:

> Unfortunately, practicing such precautions soon reaches a critical point of diminishing returns—and that is when the leaders of a democracy are so isolated from their constituents, become so much, to themselves and their supporters, mere cathode-ray figures [transparencies] rather than flesh-and-blood that the democratic process breaks down for want of genuine communication and fellow feeling. Many think we have already reached this point, but in any event that effect, if attained, would make for a powerful irony. Our assassins, who so many times have killed for their peculiar vision of liberty, would have split a cornerstone of the nation's true freedom.[18]

But if isolation is not the answer, then strict measures must be taken to safeguard the president's life during public appearances. The responsibility of protecting the president rests entirely with the U.S. Secret Service. Established in 1865, this agency's original purpose was to fight counterfeiting of America's paper money.

U.S. Secret Service agents guard President Reagan.

However, its duties changed after President William McKinley was assassinated in 1901. At that time, the public demanded that some entity be created to deal solely with presidential security. Congress decided to give the Secret Service the job of protecting McKinley's successor, Theodore Roosevelt, and in 1906 it enacted legislation making presidential protection a permanent responsibility of the agency.

Over the years the protection duties of the Secret Service have expanded, and today the agency not only safeguards the life of the president but also the vice president, the president-elect, the vice president–elect, former presidents, presidential and vice presidential candidates, visiting dignitaries, and others as directed by the president. In addition, the Secret Service guards the spouses of and children (up to age sixteen) of the president, vice president, president-elect, and vice president–elect. The agency guards the spouses and children of presidential and vice presidential candidates beginning 120 days prior to a general presidential election. The Secret Service must also protect the spouse of a deceased president until the spouse remarries.

Each person receiving Secret Service protection is permanently assigned a special detail of agents. These agents coordinate a variety of activities necessary to ensure the protectee's safety. For example, before the protectee is scheduled to appear in public, agents visit the site to survey the area, gathering information related not only to keeping the area clear of potential assassins but also to evacuating the protectee in the event of a natural disaster. They determine the location of the nearest hospital and notify local fire and rescue personnel of the impending visit. They also establish a command post with full communication facilities and coordinate the activities of law enforcement and military personnel who will aid the protection operation. The Secret Service also gathers information from law enforcement and intelligence agencies regarding any individuals or groups in the area that pose a threat to the person the agency is protecting.

A Difficult Job

Despite all precautions, as James McKinley points out, "no security plan or . . . understanding [of what makes an assassin] can forever deflect every potential killer."[19] Although the Secret Service is constantly evaluating itself to determine whether it is doing the best job possible to protect the president, it will never be possible for the agency to foresee all contingencies regarding assassination. For example, in 1972 the Secret Service was charged with protecting

Even though Governor George Wallace took many security precautions, he was shot during a campaign in 1972.

Alabama's Governor George Wallace, who was campaigning for president. Their elaborate security measures included a bulletproof podium for him to stand behind while speaking. But when Wallace unexpectedly stepped away from the podium to shake hands with members of his audience, he was shot by would-be assassin Arthur H. Bremer.

In addition, no matter how protected a president or candidate may be, the fact remains that a would-be assassin who is prepared to sacrifice his own life poses a serious threat. One example of this kind of determination occurred in October 1950, when two men tried to assassinate President Harry S. Truman, who was staying at the Blair House hotel while the White House was being remodeled. These men, Oscar Collazo and Griselio Torresola, sought to call attention to a political cause, the independence of U.S.-ruled Puerto Rico. In their attempt to kill the president, they simply walked up to the armed guards outside the hotel and opened fire, killing one and wounding two more before being shot themselves. Torresola was killed and Collazo was wounded, surviving to spend the rest of his life in prison.

Because of such incidents, the White House and the vice president's residence are well guarded by the Secret Service Uniform Division. Created in 1922 as the White House police, this division takes elaborate precautions to ensure the safety of the president while he is in the White House. Reporter Mimi Hall describes the level of security during her visit to the west wing of the White House, where the presidential offices are located:

> You approach a guarded security gate and look through the glass at three or four Secret Service agents and police officers sitting in a booth. You show them your ID and then wait outside—maybe five minutes, maybe 30—while

an agent punches your name into a computer and verifies that you have an appointment. . . .

Eventually, a buzzer sounds and you open a door. You hand over your bag or briefcase to be searched, and you proceed through a metal detector. You're given a red plastic visitor's tag on a chain to wear around your neck, instructed to keep it visible and told to head straight for the Marine at the West Wing door. . . . [Once inside] in the unlikely event that you're left alone for a moment and you go off on your own through the maze of hallways, you won't get far. Watchful eyes are literally around every corner and any visitor is likely seen by 10–20 people during any visit.

Indeed, the Secret Service won't say how many agents and police officers are stationed in the West Wing, but it's hard to turn a corner or reach the end of a hall without an agent there to look at your badge and, if you're a visitor, make sure you're with an escort. . . . [In addition, the] Secret Service acknowledges that it uses a variety of security devices to monitor what goes on.[20]

In 1999, a gunman was spotted on the roof of a building overlooking the White House. Some people suspected that he was planning to assassinate President Clinton.

But despite the best security precautions, an assassin might still find a way to reach the president, particularly since modern weaponry makes it easier to shoot from a distance. In fact, in July 1999 someone spotted a gunman on the roof of a building overlooking the White House, and some people suspect he was waiting to fire a shot when President Bill Clinton appeared outside. The man was never found, although the Secret Service acted quickly to search the area.

The future will undoubtedly hold more presidential assassination attempts. The assassin personality is marked by extreme determination given the right circumstances, and the successful assassin is a person not easily detected in a crowd. As long as the president remains accessible to the American people, his or her life will be at risk.

CHAPTER 2

The Southern Sympathizer

The first man to assassinate an American president was John Wilkes Booth, who killed Abraham Lincoln on April 14, 1865. Booth is also the only presidential assassin proven to have acted as part of a conspiracy. But although Booth did not act alone, he still exhibited the typical assassin personality. In addition, his childhood was marked by the same kind of troubles that plagued subsequent presidential assassins.

Childhood Violence

Born on May 10, 1838, John Wilkes Booth was the eighth of nine children in one of the most prominent acting families in America. His father, Junius Brutus Booth, was a British Shakespearean actor who achieved great success in the American theater. Though not married to John's mother, Junius established his family on a comfortable farming estate in Maryland and provided his children with great literature and fine art. However, he himself spent little time there. Instead, he spent months touring the United States as a theatrical performer, often accompanied by John's older brother Edwin.

Meanwhile, John remained home with his mother, who spoiled him by giving him everything he wanted while not demanding that he do any chores. Under her influence he developed a sense of entitlement and a desire for instant gratification. Known

Pampered by his mother, John Wilkes Booth quickly developed a sense of entitlement.

for being temperamental and moody, he displayed a tendency to be cruel to animals. John's violence toward animals particularly upset his father, who was so loathe to harm any living thing that he insisted his children become vegetarians. However, Junius had his own violent streak; he was an alcoholic, and when he drank he became dangerous to others. His violence became legendary after he attacked a fellow actor while on stage, stabbing the man as the theater audience looked on in horror.

Nonetheless, John envied his father's success as an actor and wanted to become one himself. But because he was unaccustomed to working for a living, young John refused to take voice or acting lessons, believing he would be good enough without them. As a result, his first performances met with poor reviews. This angered him, particularly because by that time Edwin and another brother, Junius Jr., were receiving widespread acclaim on stage.

In fact, throughout his life Booth was extremely jealous of Edwin, who was five years older than he. By 1857 Edwin was widely considered to be a major star. Consequently, when the younger Booth made his own debut in 1856, he was immediately compared to Edwin—and found lacking. It was only after Booth began acting in the South in 1858 that he earned praise for his acting ability. Southern audiences appreciated Booth's good looks and did not mind the fact that he rewrote Shakespeare's plays to include more scenes that showed off his physical agility and fencing skills.

But despite this praise, Booth continued to be jealous of Edwin's successes. According to biographer Eleanor Ruggles, although young Junius also struggled to compete with his brothers, it was John who felt really diminished by Edwin. . . . [Booth's] dream was to overthrow the Colossus [Edwin]— "I must have fame, fame." The unspoken rivalry between him and Edwin was exploited by managers. When he played in Washington the management billed him not only as the "Son of the Great Junius" but as the "Brother and Artistic Rival of Edwin Booth." The Southern press naturally

Junius Brutus Booth was upset by John's cruelty toward animals.

24

favored John. A notice of [a performance] in New Orleans boasted that "in *physique* Mr. Booth is greatly the superior of his brother Edwin, being a much handsomer and larger man, and in no other particular . . . is he at all inferior to that much-admired actor."[21]

Contempt for the President

Although this kind of praise deepened Booth's affection for the South, it could not hold him there; actors made more money and acquired more fame in the North, and Booth desperately wanted to surpass his brother Edwin in that regard. Consequently, in late 1860 Booth began performing in New York, and it was there in February 1861 that he first saw President Abraham Lincoln at a public appearance.

Booth felt nothing but contempt for the president and told his friends that Lincoln would eventually try to rule America like a king or emperor rather than a president. Booth insisted that Lincoln would someday "set up a dynasty"[22] and ruin the country. He also viewed Lincoln as an oppressor who was forcing the South to abandon its way of life by abolishing slavery. According to historian Jim Bishop, Booth "pictured the South as a land of courtly and proud people; the North, to him, was a land of crude mercenaries of enormous brute strength."[23]

Booth was jealous of the widespread acclaim that his older brother, Edwin (pictured), received.

Booth expressed contempt for all people who wanted to abolish slavery. In 1859 he had been part of a volunteer militia that hanged the famous abolitionist John Brown. After the Civil War started in 1861, Booth was an outspoken critic of the North, often alienating Northern theater audiences with his opinions. As Ruggles reports, "John, who had been acting in Albany, New York, when the [war broke out], railed at the North and praised the South so recklessly that the citizens ordered him to shut up or get out of town."[24]

Booth had adopted the South as his home in spirit if not in fact, and in his mind the South's enemies were his enemies. Despite this attitude, however, Booth did not serve in the Civil War. He told friends it was because he promised his mother he would not join the fighting, but some historians believe it was because he was afraid that a battle scar would damage his good looks. In any case, as the war progressed, Booth's hatred of Lincoln grew so intense that he expressed it at every opportunity. In 1863, for example, he denounced the president while on stage in St. Louis, Missouri. In response, police officers there detained him until he signed an oath of loyalty to the North. But the time for action, not talk, was fast approaching.

In 1864 Booth finally decided to act on his convictions. At that time, the Confederate army was desperately in need of soldiers. Booth therefore devised a plan to kidnap the president, take him to the Confederate capital of Richmond, Virginia, and ransom him for the release of over fifty thousand Confederate soldiers being held by the North. To accomplish this kidnapping, he assembled a group of coconspirators that included Confederate deserters Lewis Paine, Michael O'Laughlin, and Samuel Arnold; Confederate spy John Surratt; and George Atzerodt and David Herold, working men who had valuable information about escape routes out of Washington, D.C. O'Laughlin and Arnold were also longtime friends of Booth, and Paine was a fan of his acting.

The group met at a Washington, D.C., boardinghouse run by Surratt's mother, Mary, as well as at a tavern she operated in nearby Surrattsville, Maryland. The conspirators planned to kidnap Lincoln while he was attending a play at Ford's Theater in Washington, D.C. The plot called for one person to shut off the master gas valve in the theater, thereby extinguishing all of the lanterns. Once the theater was in darkness, Booth planned to pull a gun on the president, tie him up and gag him, and lower him over his theater box to the stage, where he would be carried outside to a waiting wagon.

Booth was a member of the group that hanged abolitionist John Brown (pictured).

26

Booth and his coconspirators had planned to kidnap Lincoln on January 18, 1865, while the president was attending a play at Ford's Theater (pictured).

Failed Kidnappings

The date of the kidnapping was set for January 18, 1865. However, Lincoln did not show up at the theater that night as planned. Some of the conspirators suspected the government might have been informed of the plan, and for two months they hid from authorities. When no one came to arrest them, they decided to try again. This time, the plan was to ambush the president's carriage while he was on his way to a play being staged at a convalescent facility called Soldier's Home. On the appointed day in March 1865, they lay in wait along the route with ropes and knives, but Lincoln never showed up. Once again they suspected that the authorities had learned of the plan, although this was not true. Lincoln had been about to leave for Soldier's Home when he changed his plan in order to speak to a regiment of soldiers instead.

Then, on April 9, 1865, the head of the Confederate army, General Robert E. Lee, surrendered to the head of the Union army, General Ulysses S. Grant. The war was effectively over. With the cause he supported lost, Booth began drinking heavily. His thoughts turned from kidnapping to killing the president, as biographer Ruggles explains:

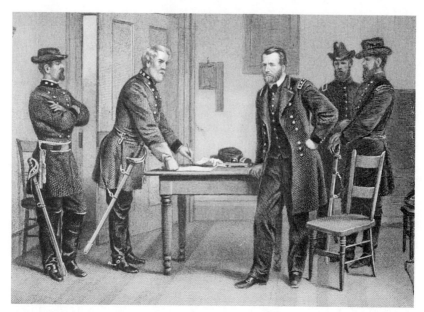

General Robert E. Lee surrenders to General Ulysses S. Grant. A devastated Booth began drinking heavily when he learned of the Yankee victory.

The ending of the War had made kidnapping the President obsolete. It was the last stroke [for Booth]: To be thus crushingly thwarted in his sacred determination to rescue the South from tyranny, and in doing so to make his name flame forever in men's minds, had set at work strange, unhappy and inherited impulses in John Wilkes Booth.[25]

Ruggles quotes one of Booth's friends, barkeeper Jack Deery, as saying that Booth's change in drinking habits was noticeable: "[Booth] now sometimes drank at my bar as much as a quart of brandy in less than two hours. . . . It was more than a spree, I could see that. . . . He seemed to be crazed by some stress of inward feeling, but only one who was very intimate with him could have told it."[26]

Booth's sister Asia later suggested that the South's defeat had somehow caused him to become mentally unbalanced: "If Wilkes Booth was mad, his mind lost its balance between the fall of Richmond and the terrific end [of the war]."[27] Others have also suggested that Booth might have gone insane right after the South fell. According to Albert Ellis and John Gullo, who have studied the assassin personality,

John Wilkes Booth . . . was commonly believed to be emotionally unbalanced. . . . In 1864 he concocted a crazy scheme to kidnap Lincoln and hand him over to the Confederate government; and his distorted enthusiasm to abduct the president grew into madness and the eventual decision to assassinate him. . . . Booth's behavior before, during, and immediately after the assassination of Lincoln would indicate that he was at the very least suffering from a temporary psychotic state; but his previous history, as well as that of various other members of his family, would lead us to suspect that he was never entirely sane.[28]

As evidence that Booth's insanity might have been lifelong, Ellis and Gullo point out that he had always been unpredictable and moody and had long been obsessed with Lincoln. However, historian Jim Bishop disagrees with this assessment, stating

He was not insane—if his acts and his conversation can be weighed psychologically—any more than another man might be called psychotic for fearing snakes or wasps to the point of becoming a nuisance on the subject. He was emotionally immature . . . but he was also shrewd and generous and a loyal friend.[29]

The Southern Cause

In a letter that Booth wrote before one of his kidnapping attempts, he outlined his reasons for his act quite rationally, even though his racist views would be considered irrational by late twentieth-century standards:

I have ever held the South were right. The very nomination of Abraham Lincoln, four years ago, plainly spoke war, war upon Southern rights and institutions. . . . The country was formed for the white, not the black man. And looking upon African slavery from the same standpoint held by the noble framers of our constitution, I, for one, have ever considered it one of the greatest blessings (both for themselves and us) that God ever bestowed upon a favored nation. Witness heretofore our wealth and our power; witness their elevation and enlightenment above their race elsewhere. . . . Lincoln's policy is only preparing a way for their total annihilation. . . . My love (as things stand today) is for the South alone. Nor do I deem it a dishonor in attempting to make for her a prisoner of this man to whom she owes so much of misery. . . . [I am] a confederate doing duty upon his own responsibility.[30]

To avenge the South, for whatever reason, Booth was determined to kill the president. He decided to commit the deed himself, but he enlisted his few remaining coconspirators to kill the vice president and the secretary of state as well in an attempt to topple the government.

Booth viewed Lincoln's policies as an infringement on the rights of the South.

By this time, all but Lewis Paine, George Atzerodt, and David Herold had left Booth's group; now that the war was over, only these three men were willing to continue supporting Booth's plans. Atzerodt accepted the responsibility of killing Vice President Andrew Johnson, and Lewis Paine and David Herold agreed to assassinating Secretary of State William H. Seward. All three murders were planned for April 14, 1865.

That night, President Lincoln and his wife were scheduled to attend a play, *Our American Cousin*, at Ford's Theater. They were to be accompanied by General Ulysses S. Grant and his wife, although in the end the Grants were unable to attend and another couple went with the Lincolns instead. Prior to the performance Booth went to the theater box where the president would sit and made sure that the lock on the box door was disabled. He then drilled a hole in the wall so he could see inside the box from its anteroom and rigged the door of the anteroom with a board that would barricade it once he was inside. In his clothes he had concealed a knife and a derringer, a small firearm that held only one bullet.

After making these preparations, Booth left the theater to wait in a saloon for the play to begin, drinking brandy and talking with friends. There, Booth issued a boast that proved to be prophetic. When someone in the bar told him, "You'll never be the actor your father was," he replied, "When I leave the stage I'll be the most famous man in America."[31]

Shortly before the performance began, Booth entered the theater through the back alley to verify that Lincoln was there. He had no trouble getting inside because he was one of Ford's regular performers. Then he left the theater again, leaving his horse in the alley; he waited until the play was more than half over, then returned through the theater's main entrance. He made his way to the president's box and discovered that, as luck would have it, the guard normally outside the box had left his post to watch the play. This eliminated the need for Booth to talk his way inside or quietly stab the guard, but although he peeked through the hole in the wall and saw Lincoln, he still did not enter the box. He was waiting for a particular moment in the play, when only one actor would be onstage. Because Booth intended to escape by jumping to the stage below, he did not want a group of actors there who could stop him.

When the key scene began, Booth entered the box, aimed his derringer at the back of the president's head, and fired. Although reports of his words vary, some witnesses said that Booth cried out "Sic semper tyrannis" ("Thus to all tyrants")[32] and "Revenge for the South!"[33] after shooting Lincoln. He also wrestled with one of the people who had accompanied Lincoln to the play, stabbing the man before leaping from the box. When he hit the stage, Booth landed hard on his left leg, breaking the bone above his ankle. Limping backstage, Booth was barely able to make his escape.

As the president watched the play, Booth stealthily approached Lincoln's box and shot the president in the back of the head.

Because Booth was so well known in the theater, many people knew who had committed the act. After the president died, angry mobs formed in the streets, harassing any Southerners they encountered as well as some of Booth's fellow actors. The public was also hostile toward Booth's relatives. In the days following the assassination, Junius Jr. and Edwin barely escaped being lynched, and every member of the family received threatening letters saying things like "we hate the name of Booth. . . . Bullets are marked for you. . . . Revolvers are loaded with which to shoot you down. . . . Your house will be burnt."[34] So intense was the harassment that Booth's mother said she hoped her son John would kill himself before the crowd got to him.

Booth's Flight

While mobs roamed the streets searching for him, Booth was making his escape, accompanied by David Herold, with whom he had rendezvoused after the assassination. Herold and Paine had gone to assassinate the secretary of state as planned; Herold waited outside the man's house with their horses as Paine went inside, beat up the secretary's assistant, and stabbed Seward. When a servant saw the commotion and called for help, Herold fled, leaving Paine to escape on his own. (The secretary later recovered from his wounds. The vice president was even more fortunate; George Atzerodt lost his nerve and could not go through with his assigned assassination.)

Booth and Herold were the targets of a massive manhunt. Soldiers blockaded roads and searched all trains leaving Washington, D.C., while detectives interviewed Booth's relatives, friends, and associates. The government also offered a substantial reward for Booth's capture. Oddly enough, Booth and Herold found that their chosen escape route, south from Maryland to Virginia, was left largely unguarded.

Booth's broken leg eventually made riding too difficult, and they stopped at the home of Samuel Mudd, a physician Booth had met during a failed real estate transaction several months earlier. Mudd set the bone, and Booth and Herold continued south. The search for the two men continued. When they neared the Maryland-Virginia border, they had to hide in woods and swamps and steal across the Potomac River by night. But Booth's injury continued to plague him, and by the time they reached the Virginia side of the Potomac on April 21, 1865, his leg had developed gangrene, a life-threatening infection.

Once in Virginia, the two sought help from Southern sympathizers, but Booth's former friends rebuffed him. Finally they found shelter in an old tobacco barn located on the farm of Richard Garrett. But the soldiers who were in pursuit soon learned of Booth's hiding place, and on the morning of April 26, 1865, at around 2:00 A.M., they surrounded the barn. When they called for the men to surrender, Herold gave himself up. Booth remained inside.

In an attempt to flush Booth out, the soldiers set fire to the barn. As the blaze grew larger, they could see Booth inside. Someone fired a gun and Booth collapsed. The soldiers dragged him out of the barn and onto the porch of Garrett's farmhouse, where he died from a bullet wound to the head. The identity of the person who fired that fatal shot is still a mystery. Several soldiers hoping for a share of the reward money claimed to have shot him, but some people believe that Booth killed himself.

The Aftermath

The manner of Booth's death is just one of several controversies that developed after the assassination. Another involves the question of whether the man killed in the barn was really Booth at all. Ever since Booth's death, some people have doubted that the man killed was really him, particularly because of the manner of his burial. Arguing that curiosity seekers might disturb the body, Secretary of War Edwin Stanton ordered it buried in secret under the stone floor

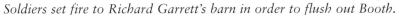

Soldiers set fire to Richard Garrett's barn in order to flush out Booth.

of a government prison. Four years later the body was moved to a Booth family plot; his relatives accepted the government's contention that it was Booth, and no one has ever proven otherwise.

Another controversy involves whether Booth was paid to kill Lincoln, and if so, whom his employer might have been. Evidence that Booth was paid is circumstantial: Booth did not make enough as an actor to support himself during the year prior to the assassination, yet there is no evidence that he was earning money elsewhere. Nonetheless, some people believe that Booth was working for the Confederacy, both because his associate John Surratt was an acknowledged Confederate spy and because Confederate documents and possible codes were found among Booth's possessions. However, scholar James McKinley argues against the view that Booth was a paid assassin for the Confederacy, saying,

> all the physical evidence, however contradictory in other ways, suggests [Booth] decided on [killing the president] independently. And *that* suggests that he was either a damned poor spy or none at all. We have our choice of motives: vanity or patriotism or congenital madness (his eccentric father . . . was called Mad Booth . . .) or as a professional hit man. . . . [And] nothing links the assassination directly to the Confederate Government.[35]

McKinley does, however, admit the possibility that someone in Lincoln's government might have hired Booth. There have been various conspiracy theories developed over the years involving Vice President Johnson, Secretary of State Seward, or Secretary of War Stanton. There was much serious public speculation after the assassination that Johnson orchestrated Lincoln's death, but modern historians tend to find the theory that Stanton was involved in Lincoln's death more plausible. This theory is based partly on the fact that Stanton received and ignored a tip that a plot against Lincoln was being planned at Mary Surratt's boardinghouse. Other Stanton decisions, such as his idea that Booth should be buried in secret and his failure to post guards along Booth's southern escape route, have also been questioned. Moreover, Stanton took possession of Booth's diary immediately after his death, and it was later discovered that eighteen pages, which covered the days just before the assassination, had been cut out.

McKinley points out that Stanton stood to benefit from Lincoln's death:

> Certainly, there is little doubt that Stanton wanted to succeed Lincoln either electorally or as the South's military dictator.

He had three major obstacles: the war, Lincoln and Johnson. The war he prolonged, then won. His accusers say he felt threatened, though, by Lincoln's growing popularity, and so he decided to strike by assassination—if not directly, then *allowing* it to happen.[36]

However, McKinley also reports that no one ever came forward, even after Stanton's death, with hard evidence of Stanton's involvement. But even if Booth was acting on behalf of Stanton, the Confederacy, or some other

Mary Surratt (pictured) was executed because of her connection to the conspirators.

person or entity, he still displayed the typical assassin personality. Moreover, Booth's actions harmed the South he supposedly loved. Lincoln's successor, Andrew Johnson, advocated much harsher policies toward Reconstruction after the Civil War, and because of Booth's Confederate connections, the North was not inclined to behave well toward Southerners after the assassination.

In addition, Booth's violent act changed the nation's perception of itself. As McKinley explains, after Lincoln's death

> what had changed was America. We had murdered our first President. . . . It was easy enough to yoke the South in recompense for Booth's act. It was less easy to regain our innocence. In the years that followed, we found it was lost forever in the mystery of ourselves. We can say that our first assassination was our hardest. After Lincoln, we knew how.[37]

As for what became of Booth's coconspirators, several soon followed him to the grave. Herold and Paine were tried and hanged for their attempt to kill the secretary of state, as was Atzerodt for his intent to kill the vice president. Mary Surratt was also executed, even though she claimed not to have known about the conspiracy being hatched in her house. The remaining conspirators all served time in prison for plotting to kidnap Lincoln, as did Samuel Mudd, the physician who treated Booth's injured leg.

John Surratt was not put on trial until June 10, 1867, two years after Lincoln's death. Immediately after the assassination he had fled to Canada, then to England, Italy, and finally Egypt, where he was arrested and brought back to the United States. Once back in America, he was charged with murder, largely because two witnesses claimed to have seen him with Booth at the theater shortly before the president was killed. However, Surratt insisted that he had been in Elmira, New York, at that time, and during the trial his attorneys presented several witnesses who placed Surratt in New York. The prosecution countered with still other witnesses who swore they had seen Surratt in Washington, D.C.

In all, ninety witnesses testified for the defense and eighty for the prosecution, and the trial lasted two months. But in the end, the jury could not come to an agreement on Surratt's guilt; four people voted him guilty and eight not guilty. Eventually the government decided not to retry the case, and Surratt was released from jail in the summer of 1868. He then became a teacher and sometimes lectured about his former association with John Wilkes Booth, but until his death in 1916 he insisted that he had played no part in Lincoln's murder.

CHAPTER 3

A Disgruntled Office Seeker

Like John Wilkes Booth, Charles Julius Guiteau had an apparent political motive for shooting President James A. Garfield on July 2, 1881. Guiteau blamed Garfield for a rift that had developed within the Republican Party and believed his assassination would somehow benefit the party and the country. However, Guiteau also had a personal motive for killing the president: Garfield had repeatedly refused to give Guiteau a job. This refusal was just one in a series of disappointments for Guiteau that added to the anger he kept inside himself.

A Difficult Childhood

Born in Freeport, Illinois, on September 8, 1841, Guiteau had a difficult life from the beginning. He was his mother's third child, and after he was born she fell into a severe depression that worsened with the birth of two more children, each of whom died in infancy; she herself died when Guiteau was seven years old. Guiteau's father, a local politician, was an opinionated man and religious zealot who beat his children for the slightest transgression. He criticized Charles for wanting to buy things he could not afford, and the two quarreled over this and many other matters. By the time Charles was twelve years old, the relationship between father and son was so bad that he was sent to live with his older sister and her husband in Chicago.

The boy remained with them until he was sixteen, whereupon

Charles Julius Guiteau's victim was President James A. Garfield (pictured).

he returned to Freeport to try once more to live with his father, who had remarried. A year later he left home again, this time to attend college in Ann Arbor, Michigan. But before he could start classes at the University of Michigan, the school administration discovered that Guiteau did not have the requisite high-school background to attend. As a result, Guiteau's acceptance to the university was revoked.

A Religious Conversion

Left with no plans for the future, Guiteau felt frustrated and aimless until he decided to embrace the religious teachings he remembered from his childhood. Guiteau's father had been a follower of the Reverend John Humphrey Noyes, a self-proclaimed Christian Perfectionist, and after reading Noyes's book *The Berean*, Guiteau decided to become a Christian Perfectionist, too.

Noyes preached that Jesus Christ did not intend for people to sin and then repent; instead, Christ wanted people to live perfect lives on Earth. Moreover, Noyes believed that the return of Christ to Earth, an event known as the Second Coming, had not only been predicted in the Bible but had already come to pass in A.D. 70. At that time, Noyes suggested, Christ encouraged people to work together to create a heaven on Earth, where sinless perfection was the norm. To help his followers achieve this perfection, Noyes established a collective farm for them in New York State. Called the Oneida Community, its approximately three hundred members referred to themselves as "Bible communists" and lived according to Noyes's principles.

One of these principles was the "complex marriage," whereby all men in the group were considered married to all women in the group. Noyes believed that in heaven, everyone loved everyone else, so there could be no such thing as an exclusive relationship between two people. For the same reason, in the Oneida Community all of the adults were considered the parents of all of the group's children.

In addition, all money, goods, and chores were shared equally in the community. Every person worked hard to run the collective farm and to produce various items for sale to the general public. These items included furniture, leather suitcases, palm-leaf hats, wheel spokes, and steel animal traps.

Members of the Oneida Community also engaged in "mutual criticism," meeting in groups to openly criticize one another. People were encouraged to point out each other's faults as a way to help the group as a whole achieve perfection. Raised by a perfectionist father, this aspect of the community appealed to Guiteau, who moved to Oneida at the age of nineteen.

Within a few weeks, however, Guiteau had grown to hate the criticism sessions. He was also upset because the women in the community did not find him attractive. Moreover, he disliked doing farm chores, partly because he was not as good at them as other community members. Frustrated with his inadequacies, he found himself wanting to leave Oneida, but by this time the Civil War had broken out, and Guiteau feared that if he left he would be drafted into the Union army. Therefore, he remained in the community until the war's end. However, he spent much of his time complaining to Noyes about his job assignments and the way the group was run. One official church letter, sent to Guiteau's father in 1865, suggested that the young man was displaying some mental instability:

> [Guiteau] has manifested a decided repugnance to labor with his hands, and indeed to business of all kinds, claiming for himself the privileges of a student. . . . He wrote Mr. Noyes a long communication, in which he was very insolent, charging him with tyranny and oppression. . . . The truth about the matter is that we consider that there is . . . much evidence of an unsound insane mind in all of this.[38]

More Failures

With the end of the Civil War in April 1865, Guiteau finally left Oneida. He went to New York City intending to establish a daily religious newspaper, but he could find no one willing to invest in the project. He returned to Oneida a failure.

Within months he left again, this time to work as a law clerk in Chicago. Now certain that he was finished with the Oneida Community, Guiteau tried to make them pay him $9,150 as compensation for the work he had done for the community while living there. He also wanted Noyes to return $700 of an inheritance that he had contributed to the community upon joining. In one of his letters demanding his inheritance money, Guiteau wrote, "If I had never gone to the Oneida Community, by this time (in all human probability) I should have had a good law practice, and a nice family, and other things to match, but now I have neither."[39]

Guiteau never received his money. Nonetheless, in 1868 he opened his own legal practice, specializing in the collection of overdue bills. Ironically, Guiteau was notorious for leaving his own bills unpaid. He would stay in a rented room for weeks without settling his debts, then leave just when the landlord was threatening him with legal action.

Not long after this, in 1869, Guiteau got married on an impulse. His bride was a sixteen-year-old librarian named Annie Bunn, and from the beginning Guiteau did not love her. He told friends that he should never have married Bunn, and he admitted doing so after knowing her only ten hours. He displayed a violent temper, beating his wife frequently. In addition, he visited prostitutes throughout his marriage; this adultery made it legally possible for his wife to divorce him in 1874.

By then Guiteau had experienced yet another failure. In 1872 he had moved to New York City to support the Democratic presidential candidacy of Horace Greeley, believing that if Greeley won he would give Guiteau a political appointment. Perhaps his desire to hold office was related to the fact that his father was a politician, or perhaps it stemmed from Guiteau's belief that the job was easy and paid well. In either case, when Greeley lost, Guiteau was crushed; he had already been practicing his acceptance speech and had purchased clothes befitting the job he was certain he would receive.

Democratic presidential candidate Horace Greeley.

After this disappointment Guiteau continued working as a bill collector in New York. To increase his income, he cheated his clients, taking a slightly larger fee than was customary each time he collected on an overdue bill. He also cheated debtors, telling them that he was unable to collect on a bill when in fact he had gotten the money and kept it for himself. Eventually a New York newspaper, the *Herald,* exposed Guiteau's thievery. Guiteau sued the newspaper for libel but dropped the suit and fled to Chicago when a client stepped forward to substantiate the accusation.

His Father's Footsteps

Once back in Chicago, Guiteau decided to try making a living as a preacher. Although he possessed no credentials or training as a minister, in 1877 he drew on his experiences at the Oneida Community to write a speech on the Second Coming of Jesus Christ. He then rented a hall for a night and advertised his speech in local newspapers. Admission to the event would be free, but a donation was requested of those who could afford to make one. Of the thirty people who showed up to hear the speech, only a handful paid; Guiteau earned less than two dollars. Nonetheless, over the next two years Guiteau continued to give religious speeches, charging money for his appearances and supplementing his income by selling insurance. He was described by most people during this time as a poor speaker. In reviewing one of his lectures, a newspaper reporter said,

> Is There a Hell? Fifty Deceived People [are] of the opinion that there ought to be. The man Charles J. Guiteau, if such really is his name, who calls himself an eminent Chicago lawyer, has fraud and imbecility plainly stamped upon his countenance. . . . Although the impudent scoundrel had talked only fifteen minutes, he suddenly perorated [concluded] brilliantly by thanking the audience for their attention and bidding them good-night. Before the astounded fifty had recovered from their amazement . . . [he] had fled from the building and escaped.[40]

In 1879, in an attempt to make more money without putting in much effort, Guiteau self-published his talks in a book entitled *The Truth: A Companion to the Bible*. The ideas in the book were hardly original; its contents were strikingly similar to those in Noyes's *The Berean*. But although Guiteau hoped otherwise, his work failed to bring him the fame or wealth he craved.

In search of fame, Guiteau decided to become a politician. Disillusioned by Greeley's failed Democratic candidacy, Guiteau switched party affiliation and became a Republican. He also became a supporter of General Ulysses S. Grant, who was running against James A. Garfield for the Republication nomination for

Republican presidential candidate Ulysses S. Grant.

General Winfield Scott Hancock.

president. When Garfield won the nomination, Guiteau became a Garfield supporter.

Convinced that he could sway voters to support the Republican Party, Guiteau wrote a speech opposing the economic policies advocated by the Democratic candidate, General Winfield Scott Hancock, who was arguing that the South needed more economic assistance to rebuild after the Civil War. Guiteau showed his speech to Garfield's campaign leaders in New York, expecting them to offer him a paid position as a political speaker. When they refused to hire him, Guiteau gave his speech without their sanction to anyone who would listen.

In an attempt to increase his audience, Guiteau also printed copies of his speech and passed them out to voters. These pamphlets were mostly ignored by those who saw them, but when Garfield won the presidency, Guiteau was convinced that his speech was responsible for the victory. Guiteau now felt that Garfield owed him a favor. He wrote the newly elected president a letter saying he wanted a political appointment because "we have cleaned them out,"[41] meaning that together Guiteau and Garfield had vanquished the Democrats. Guiteau asked that, in return for his help, he be named the U.S. consul in Vienna, Austria.

Demanding Payment

Garfield had never met Guiteau, and there is no evidence that he answered the letter. Failing to receive a reply, Guiteau sent more letters. In one of his subsequent messages, he falsely claimed that he was getting married, believing that Garfield would be more likely to make him a consul if he had a wife. In another, he changed his request and asked for a position as consul in Paris, saying that he had decided he preferred Paris to Vienna.

Garfield ignored all of Guiteau's letters, and finally Guiteau decided to talk to the president in person. In March 1881 he traveled to Washington, D.C., went to the White House, and personally gave Garfield a copy of his speech. Across the top of the document Guiteau had written his name and his desired position: consul in Paris. Garfield politely accepted the speech but made no promises.

On March 11, the day after visiting the president, Guiteau left a copy of his speech for Secretary of State James Blaine, along with a letter asking for the French consulship and stating that his speech was responsible for Garfield's election. Fourteen days later, Guiteau again wrote to Blaine. The following day, having received no response, he wrote to Garfield claiming that Blaine supported his appointment as a consul to France. Again he received no response. Despite being ignored, he continued to badger both Garfield and Blaine with letters, which he hand delivered to their offices until their secretaries eventually had him barred from the premises. He also left letters for other prominent people in Congress and the State Department, hoping they could influence the president.

As days passed and no appointment materialized, Guiteau grew more and more angry over his situation. Then Garfield did something that triggered Guiteau to change from a spurned office seeker into a political zealot. The president made a controversial political appointment that ignited criticism from editorialists as well as some fellow Republicans.

Stalwarts and Half-Breeds

At that time, the Republicans were split into two factions, known as the Stalwarts and the Half-Breeds. Garfield was a Half-Breed, as was Blaine. The vice president, Chester A. Arthur, was a Stalwart; he had been chosen for the position specifically to help heal the division in the party. But when Garfield gave an important appointment—New York customs collector—to a Half-Breed, the Stalwarts became incensed. In fact, the two Stalwart senators from New York resigned their offices in protest, accusing Garfield's administration of favoring the Half-Breeds. Newspaper columnists suggested that this favoritism would bring ruin on both the Republican Party and the nation.

When Guiteau heard these attacks on Garfield, he concluded that the president had to die for the

Vice President Chester A. Arthur.

good of the country. He later wrote, "This is not a murder. It is a political necessity. . . . [It will] save the republic."[42] He also described how he arrived at his decision:

> [I was] greatly depressed in mind and spirit from the political situation, and I should say it was about half past eight, before I had gone to sleep, when an impression came over my mind like a flash that if the President was out of the way, this whole thing would be solved and everything would go well. That is the first impression I had with reference to removing the President.[43]

Within days Guiteau began to think of his "impression" as being sent to him by God. But before acting on his idea, he tried to ruin the career of Secretary of State Blaine, as punishment for Blaine's failure to respond to his letters. On May 23, 1881, Guiteau sent a letter to Garfield saying, "Mr. Blaine is a wicked man, and you ought to demand his *immediate* resignation; otherwise, you and the Republican Party will come to grief."[44]

Two weeks later, Guiteau bought a gun. He chose the most impressive-looking weapon he could find, believing it would someday hold a place of honor in a museum. Then he set out to learn how to shoot. He practiced in the woods every day, and when he felt competent enough with the weapon, he began stalking the president. On at least three occasions he almost shot Garfield but changed his mind because the circumstances were not perfect. Guiteau wanted everything, including the weather, to be just right, since the incident would be retold in the history books.

At the Train Depot

Finally, on July 2, 1881, Guiteau decided to act. He had heard that Garfield would be taking a train from Washington, D.C., to New England that day, boarding at the Baltimore and Ohio Railroad Depot. Guiteau arose early in the morning on the day of the president's scheduled departure, dressed in his best clothes, and went to the depot, where he hired a carriage. He told the driver that he wanted to be taken from the depot to a nearby cemetery, and he asked the man to wait for him. Guiteau later said that he did not intend to escape in the carriage and that he planned to turn himself in to the police shortly after shooting the president. However, he feared that an angry mob would form at the depot after the assassination, and he wanted to avoid harm to himself.

Garfield arrived at the depot shortly after Guiteau, at 9:20 A.M. The president was accompanied by Secretary of State Blaine. Guiteau watched the two men walk through one waiting room before coming up behind them in another and shooting Garfield, first in the back and then in the arm. Guiteau then dashed outside for the carriage, but before he could reach it, a policeman arrested him. As he was taken into custody, he said: "Arthur is President, and I am a Stalwart."[45]

Guiteau's remark led some people to conclude that he was a member of a Stalwart conspiracy to kill the president. Others believed that the Democrats were behind the attack, or Southern rebels, or socialists. But investigators who interviewed Guiteau in jail quickly decided that he had acted alone and that he had mental problems. Edward C. Spitzka, a neurologist who examined Guiteau shortly after the shooting and later testified at his trial, said,

> A thorough study will convince an impartial and competent jury of medical examiners, before whom such a case should

On July 2, 1881, Guiteau shot Garfield from behind in a train depot.

be laid, that Guiteau is not only now insane, but that he has never been anything else. . . . The marked feature of this man's insanity is a tendency toward delusive opinion, and to the creation of morbid or fantastical projects. . . . There is a marked element of imbecility of judgment.[46]

Spitzka further noted that five of Guiteau's relatives, including an uncle and two aunts, had histories of mental illness; therefore, he concluded that the man was not responsible for his actions, saying, "His insanity is not the result of his own vices, but based on defective organization inherited from a diseased ancestry."[47] Even Garfield, lying on his deathbed, made his own diagnosis of Guiteau: "He must have been crazy."[48]

On Trial for Murder

Garfield lingered eighty days before dying. His arm wound was not serious, but the bullet he took in his back had lodged itself deep inside his body. Doctors were not sure where to find it, but they suspected that it was in the stomach or pancreas. One after another, they poked and prodded into the wound with unsterile

President Garfield suffered from infection and high fever for eighty days before dying.

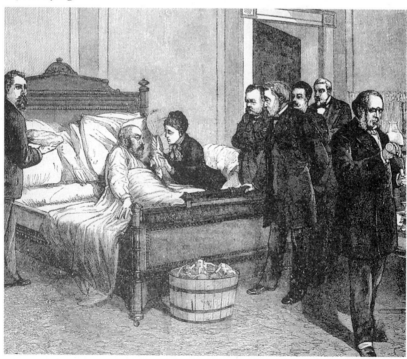

fingers. Massive infection soon followed. Garfield suffered from a high fever and grew increasingly weaker. Nonetheless, doctors performed exploratory surgery in yet another failed attempt to find the bullet. This spread the infection still farther and caused additional internal damage from which the president never recovered. Garfield died on September 19, 1881.

At the time of his death, doctors believed that a blood vessel near the bullet had ruptured, but in fact Garfield had suffered heart failure as a result of his infection. Moreover, when an autopsy was performed, the medical examiner discovered that the bullet had lodged itself four inches from the spine and that Garfield's immune system had encased it in a protective cyst. Many people, including Guiteau himself, believed that Garfield would have survived if the doctors had not tried to remove the bullet.

At his murder trial, which took place two months after Garfield's death, Guiteau argued that he was not to blame for the president's demise, the doctors were. Moreover, Guiteau clearly behaved irrationally in the courtroom. As scholar Justus D. Doenecke reports,

> Guiteau acted as a most peculiar defendant, interrogating prospective jurors on biblical doctrines, shouting at hostile witnesses, and in general implying that he spoke for the Deity. He told the court that during the 1880 [presidential campaign] he "used to go to General Arthur [the vice presidential candidate] and talk just as freely with him as I would with anybody"; he did admit, however, that no Republican leader had ever acknowledged his desire to aid the party.[49]

The trial went on for eleven weeks, as Guiteau's lawyers argued with prosecutors over whether their client was sane at the time of the murder. Even those who knew him best disagreed on his sanity. Annie Bunn, Guiteau's former wife, testified that he was sane while she knew him; on the other hand, Guiteau's father wrote a letter to the court saying his son had always belonged in a mental institution. Toward the end of the trial, Guiteau himself testified that he was insane during the shooting.

Meanwhile, Guiteau's courtroom antics had convinced some people that he was indeed mentally ill, but most assumed he was faking insanity to avoid a guilty verdict. The public generally believed that Guiteau had killed the president out of anger because he had been denied a political appointment.

McKinley notes that prosecutors sometimes engaged in trickery to promote this view: "Despite having the acknowledged killer in jail, the state's lawyers coached witnesses on their testimony and bribed some experts to testify that Guiteau was, [by an existing legal definition], sane. They suppressed or destroyed letters and documents that might show that he was crazy."[50]

No Mercy

The efforts to prove Guiteau insane were to no avail. On January 25, 1882, after only an hour of deliberation, the jury found Guiteau sane and guilty of Garfield's murder. The assassin was immediately sentenced to hang. Over the next few weeks, Guiteau's lawyers appealed this verdict, but they failed to win him a new trial or a more lenient sentence. Upon considering the prospect of mercy for Guiteau, U.S. attorney general Benjamin Harris Brewster argued against a presidential pardon, saying that to allow Guiteau to live would "shake the public confidence in the certainty and justice of the courts."[51]

The new president, Chester Arthur, agreed with this position and refused to stay Guiteau's execution; the convicted assassin

Failing to convince the jury that he was insane when he assassinated Garfield, Guiteau was found guilty and sentenced to hang.

was hanged on June 30, 1882. There are various accounts of his last words, which were heard by some three hundred witnesses. Some reports say that he died singing a religious poem he had written himself. Others quote his last words as being "I saved my party and my land, Glory hallelujah!"[52]

After Guiteau's death, an autopsy revealed some abnormalities in his brain, possibly caused by a sexually transmitted disease. Guiteau's skeleton was prepared for public display, but before it was exhibited, government officials decided against such a spectacle. The location of Guiteau's bones is unknown, although many believe that they are stored in an army medical museum.

The Aftermath

Guiteau's act of assassination had two important consequences. First, it inspired reforms in the way people received federal jobs. The president's power to fill certain positions was reduced, and the Civil Service Commission was established to make certain appointments to government jobs. Second, after the assassination there was a change in attitude regarding the safety of the president. Most people began to question whether the leader of the nation should be easily accessible to the public. However, little was done to make it more difficult to kill a president, and twenty years later another assassin struck with as much ease as Guiteau.

CHAPTER 4

The Anarchist

The third person to assassinate a president was Leon Czolgosz, an avowed anarchist who shot William McKinley on September 6, 1901. Like John Wilkes Booth and Charles Guiteau, Czolgosz attributed the assassination to a political motive, but also like them his act was triggered by a desire to feel important.

A Childhood of Hard Work

Czolgosz could not have envisioned himself achieving the kind of success that a U.S. president enjoyed. Born in 1873 in Detroit, Michigan, he grew up in poverty as the fourth of eight children, six of whom were boys. His parents emigrated to the United States from Poland just weeks before Leon was born, and his father worked as a common laborer on such projects as building sewer systems. His mother was a laundress, but she died when Leon was twelve due to complications in the birth of her eighth child.

Left with an infant and seven other children to care for, Czolgosz's father soon remarried. He also moved his family from one Michigan town to another, then to Pittsburgh, Pennsylvania, and later to Cleveland, Ohio, as he followed construction jobs. Wherever he was, he sent his sons out to work to help support the family. Eventually the boys contributed enough income to buy a saloon in a run-down area of Cleveland as well as a fifty-five-acre farm just outside of town.

Leon Czolgosz grew up in poverty as the fourth of eight children.

50

Czolgosz went to work when he was only sixteen, having completed just five and a half years of schooling. His first job was at a Pittsburgh bottle factory. When he was eighteen, he started working at a Cleveland wire mill, a job he would hold until he was twenty-five years old.

Becoming an Anarchist

During his years at the mill, Czolgosz became interested in the socialist and anarchist philosophies promoted by some labor activists working there. Socialists hold the view that property, goods, and income should be controlled by social groups rather than by profit-motivated individuals and institutions. They believe that people should live cooperatively, working together for the common good, and have historically opposed rule by elite classes.

However, while socialists disagree on how a cooperative social system should be created, they generally believe that the government must first be taken over by socialists before any change can occur. In contrast, anarchists believe that anyone who achieves power will quickly become corrupted by that power and will therefore become as evil as the rulers he or she sought to replace. In fact, anarchists are opposed to all forms of social control—not only governments but also churches, laws, the military, and financial institutions. As anarchist Liz A. Highleyman explains,

> Anarchists generally believe that human beings are capable of managing their own affairs on the basis of creativity, cooperation, and mutual respect. It is believed that power is inherently corrupting, and that authorities are inevitably more concerned with self-perpetuation and increasing their own power than they are with doing what is best for their constituents.[53]

Czolgosz attended socialist meetings while working at the mill, and in 1893 he participated in a socialist-led labor strike in an attempt to increase wages. The strike was lengthy and brought disappointing results. Afterward, when Czolgosz returned to his job, he began using an assumed name—Fred C. Nieman (a surname meaning "No Man" or "Nobody" in German)—because he feared that someone in the company or the government would persecute him for his participation in the strike.

Changes in Behavior

As part of his interest in anarchism, Czolgosz began to question his faith. He had been raised a Roman Catholic, but since anarchists are opposed to organized religion, he stopped going to church. He spent his spare time working, going to meetings of radical groups, and hanging out in saloons.

To observers, Czolgosz would have seemed like just another millworker. But in 1898 something happened to Czolgosz that did not fit the millworker's lifestyle. Then twenty-five years old, he suddenly experienced an episode of mental illness whereby he became reclusive and moody. He abruptly quit his job and went to live on his family's farm. There, he slept long hours, did very few chores, and avoided people as much as possible, eating meals alone in his room. When he had any contact at all with his family, he usually fought with them and railed against the American government.

It was rumored that anarchists were planning to kill every major world ruler, including the czar of Russia (pictured).

Czolgosz grew particularly agitated after reading anarchist newspapers. When he read about the assassination of the king of Italy, he clipped out the newspaper article and kept it with him at all times, even when he slept. Around this time, reports were surfacing that anarchists were plotting to kill every major world ruler, including either the queen of England or the prince of Wales, the czar of Russia, and the president of the United States. In April 1900 the prince of Wales barely escaped an assassin's bullet; following this attack, the American public grew concerned about their own leader's safety. As Margaret Leech explains in her book *In the Days of McKinley,*

> The rich and peaceful landscape of the national life seemed undermined by violence. Assassination was an un-American crime, and Americans did not care to think about it. They liked the idea that their Chief Executives behaved like ordinary citizens, going freely about their occasions, sitting in a theater or walking through a railway station. Now, in guilty confusion, men asked themselves if another President were to follow Lincoln and Garfield.[54]

In response to these concerns, the government assigned a guard to the current president, William McKinley, but McKinley often went off without the man. As Leech reports, "McKinley lived, as far as possible, like a private citizen. He continued to walk unattended to church or the business district. At Washington, he often slipped off for a stroll in the White House grounds. . . . He remained utterly—perhaps fatalistically—indifferent to warnings of physical danger."[55]

An Abrupt Departure

Meanwhile, Czolgosz tried to get help for his mental illness. He went to several doctors in Cleveland and was given medication but only became more moody and argumentative. He also continued to sleep long hours.

Then, in early 1901, Czolgosz suddenly decided that he had to get away from his family. He demanded that his father give him back the money he had earned over the years, or at least the portion that had been used to buy the family farm. His father refused to pay him anything, but Czolgosz did not let the matter die. He continued to badger his family with requests for money, and finally, in July 1901, he was given a small sum. He immediately went to Chicago in an attempt to meet a famous anarchist, Emma Goldman.

Just two months earlier, Czolgosz had gone to one of Goldman's lectures in Cleveland. Originally from Russia, Goldman had been involved with American socialists and anarchists for more than fifteen years. When Czolgosz tried to meet her in Chicago, she was running to catch a train and would not talk to him. He contacted other anarchists around this time as well, but they, too, snubbed him; Czolgosz's strange behavior caused them to suspect him of being a spy for the government. But despite the snubs, Czolgosz still wanted to be a part of the anarchist movement; some scholars believe that it was at this point that he decided to kill the president as a way to gain the acceptance he craved.

Going to the Exposition

A few days after attempting to meet with Goldman, Czolgosz moved to Buffalo, New York, the

Czolgosz attempted to meet anarchist Emma Goldman (pictured).

site of a fair called the Pan-American Exposition. Its purpose was to showcase the people and technology of the United States, and for several weeks prior to the fair's opening in May 1901, newspapers had been reporting that President McKinley would attend.

At first Czolgosz stayed in a boardinghouse just outside of town, but on August 31 he rented a room over a saloon in Buffalo using the name John Doe. Little is known about his activities at this time, but what is certain is that on September 2 he bought a short-barreled .32-caliber revolver for $4.50.

On September 5, by his own account, Czolgosz attended a speech given by McKinley at the exposition before a crowd of approximately fifty thousand people. The next day, he followed McKinley on a tour of nearby Niagara Falls, and at 4:00 P.M. he went to a reception in the Temple of Music, a building at the exposition, where McKinley had agreed to spend ten minutes shaking hands with members of the public.

With a handkerchief wrapped around his right hand to conceal the revolver he held, Czolgosz patiently waited in line to meet the president. McKinley was guarded by about fifty people, but none

Czolgosz's victim, President William McKinley, delivers a speech before a crowd in Quincy, Illinois.

of them thought it strange that someone would have his hand wrapped that way. To allay suspicion, Czolgosz would periodically raise his hand and pretend to wipe sweat from his forehead with the handkerchief. One of the president's guards, however, thought that Czolgosz's hand was bandaged in an unusual enough way to attract his attention. In a newspaper interview shortly after the event, a Secret Service agent identified as Mr. Ireland reported that

> a few moments before Czolgosz approached, a man had come along with three fingers of his right hand tied in a bandage and he had shaken hands with his left. When Czolgosz came up I noticed that he was a boyish-looking fellow with an innocent face, perfectly calm, and I also noticed that his right hand was wrapped in what appeared to be a bandage. I watched him closely, but was interrupted by the man who was in front of him, who held onto the President's hand an unusually long time. This man . . . was persistent and it was necessary for me to push him along somewhat so that the others could reach the President.[56]

Shots Fired

At this point, the president had been shaking hands for approximately seven minutes. When Czolgosz reached him, McKinley extended his hand to shake Czolgosz's, but Czolgosz pushed it aside and fired twice. The blast ignited his handkerchief, and the hall fell silent. Then the president put his right hand under his coat and grimaced. At the same time, Ireland grabbed Czolgosz by the left arm, and the next person in line behind Czolgosz struck the gunman in the neck with one hand and made a grab for the revolver with the other. Others in the assembly then knocked Czolgosz to the floor, whereupon he again tried to fire the revolver. Someone struck his arm, the gun slid across the floor, and a soldier picked it up and put it in his pocket.

As the mob piled on top of Czolgosz, President McKinley, who was being led to a chair, exclaimed, "Don't let them hurt him."[57] Czolgosz was dragged away from the crowd and into another room before being taken to Buffalo's police headquarters.

Despite McKinley's request that Czolgosz not be hurt, the assassin was beaten nearly to death by some of the president's guards and by members of the military escort that took him to jail. An angry crowd gathered outside the jail and the state militia was ordered into readiness

Czolgosz, with his .32-caliber revolver wrapped in a handkerchief, assassinates President McKinley.

to protect the prisoner from being lynched. Even with the precautions, many people doubted whether Czolgosz would survive to stand trial.

A Failed Operation

After the shooting McKinley had been taken to the Pan-American Exposition's "emergency hospital," which was actually more like a nurse's office with dim lighting. There, two surgeons operated on the president to try to find the bullet. One of the shots had been deflected by McKinley's ribs; that bullet was discovered in the president's clothes. The other had gone through his stomach and lodged somewhere else in his body, but doctors could not find it.

Ironically, one of the modern inventions being displayed at the exposition was an early X-ray machine, but the doctors did not trust or understand the device and refused to use it to help them find the bullet. They also failed to drain blood that was pooling within the injured area of the body. Instead, they simply closed the wound after trying to repair the damage the bullet had caused to the stomach.

When the operation was over, McKinley was taken to the home of the exposition president, Mr. Milburn. At first, doctors were certain McKinley would recover, and they issued several news bulletins to that effect. But on the seventh day after the operation, the president's health suddenly worsened. Despite the doctors' precautions regarding sanitation, gangrene had set in along the path of the bullet, which had not only passed through the stomach but also through the pancreas and a kidney. McKinley died the next day.

A Speedy Trial

Czolgosz was now a murderer. On September 17, 1901, he was transferred to a prison in Auburn, New York, were he would remain during his trial. While he was being transferred, a mob attacked and beat him so severely that he could not walk. Doubled over with severe pain, he had to be dragged and carried to his new jail cell.

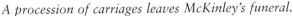

A procession of carriages leaves McKinley's funeral.

When he had first been arrested, Czolgosz stated that he was an anarchist and a "disciple" of Emma Goldman, and his beliefs in this regard were the reason he killed the president. He saw it as his "duty" to do so. During his trial, he continued to insist that he had assassinated McKinley purely for the anarchist cause. At one point he said, "I don't believe one man should have so much service. . . . I thought it would be a good thing for the country to kill the President."[58] Czolgosz further stated that he had acted alone and was not paid to assassinate McKinley.

Czolgosz refused to claim insanity, refused the help of his lawyers, and refused to say anything else in his own defense. As a result, his trial lasted only eight and a half hours, and the jury deliberated for only a half hour. Czolgosz was determined to be, in the words of the court, "the product of anarchy, sane and responsible"[59] and found guilty. He was sentenced to die in the electric chair on October 29, 1901.

On that date, Czolgosz was led twenty feet down the hall from his cell to the execution room. As he was being strapped into the chair, he said, "I killed the President because he was the enemy of the good people—the good working people. I am not sorry for my crime."[60] He was then hit with seventeen hundred volts of electricity for one full minute, and it was clear afterward that he was dead. The hatred Czolgosz's crime aroused is indicated by the fact that a prison official suggested that Czolgosz be given another jolt for good measure despite the fact that he was already dead. The electricity was turned back on for another full minute of seventeen hundred volts, and after it was turned off again, the assassin was finally officially pronounced dead.

The same hatred that prison officials expressed for Czolgosz continued after his death. When his body was placed in its coffin, someone poured sulfuric acid over the corpse. This would hasten its decay and was also an expression of contempt.

The Aftermath

Czolgosz's act of assassination had several effects on the nation. Shortly after McKinley's successor, Theodore Roosevelt, took over the office, he made the Secret Service fully responsible for the president's protection. This protection was to be full-time, regardless of any president's complaints. As scholar James McKinley puts it, "It had taken Lincoln, Garfield and McKinley, but now professional security men would guard the Chief Executive."[61]

In addition, doctors began to reexamine the issue of insanity and its relationship to assassination. Although Czolgosz's brain had

Deeply affected by the assassination of McKinley, President Theodore Roosevelt (pictured) put the Secret Service in charge of protecting him.

been removed and autopsied, no signs of abnormality had been found. Consequently, they looked for evidence in Czolgosz's background that might help them understand why he might have become an assassin. Similarly, legal experts studied the case to better determine how to defend assassins in court. Despite his statements and behavior at the trial, these doctors and lawyers came to believe that Czolgosz had been insane since it became clear that he had not really been as much a part of the anarchist movement as he had claimed. They also discovered that he had sought treatment for mental illness and concluded that this fact should have been presented at his trial.

Ironically, Czolgosz's act caused immediate and serious problems for those he claimed to care about: the working classes in general and anarchists in particular. The president's death brought on a financial crisis in the nation that weakened many businesses and caused the layoff of many workers. Businesses also persecuted anarchists. As James McKinley reports,

> There was a Wall Street [financial] panic and an immense antianarchist wave. Employers fired and mobs attacked known anarchists. [Emma] Goldman and others were arrested, abused and threatened before proving they were innocent of McKinley's death. Paterson, New Jersey . . . was targeted for sacking, since it was a notorious anarchist stronghold, full of working stiffs and other low types—but authorities intervened [and saved the town from destruction].[62]

It was difficult for people to accept that a lone gunman could have planned and committed such a deed. Regardless of Czolgosz's claims, many people believed that he had not acted alone. They blamed other anarchists for the president's death, certain there had been a conspiracy to kill McKinley.

The Lone Gunman—or Conspirator?

The presidential assassination that generated the most conspiracy theories was that of John F. Kennedy, who was killed on November 22, 1963. The man accused of committing the crime was Lee Harvey Oswald, and like previous presidential assassins, Oswald possessed both strong political beliefs and deep feelings of inadequacy and frustration, having grown up under difficult circumstances.

Childhood Problems

Born in New Orleans on October 18, 1939, Oswald never knew his father, an insurance agent who died right before he was born. This death had a devastating effect on Oswald's mother, Marguerite, because she had planned to remain at home to care for Lee Harvey; his five-year-old brother, Robert; and his seven-year-old half brother, John Pic. Instead, she had to get a job to support herself and her family.

Once she was working, Marguerite found it too difficult to care for her three sons, so she sent her older two children to live at an orphanage. Relatives and neighbors looked after Lee Harvey until he was three, whereupon he was sent to the orphanage as well. A year later, Marguerite brought her children back home in anticipation of her marriage to Edwin A. Ekdahl, which took place in May

Three police photographs of Lee Harvey Oswald.

1945. But once again Marguerite found her children too much of a burden; that fall she sent her older two sons away to a military academy. Lee Harvey remained at home. He grew very attached to Ekdahl, but Marguerite and her new husband fought constantly over a wide variety of issues. The two separated several times and finally divorced in 1948. According to John Pic, the main reason for the divorce was money; Marguerite constantly criticized Ekdahl for not giving her more.

After the divorce, Marguerite worked in a series of jobs, including insurance sales. Oswald often waited in the car while she called on clients. During the school year, he always came home to an empty house, and his mother forbade him to go outside unless she was home. As a result, he spent a great deal of time by himself.

Neglected and upset over his mother's divorce, Oswald became an angry, difficult teen. He often skipped school and twice threatened relatives with a knife. He also sometimes struck his mother, who often complained about how unfairly life had treated her. She still felt that having children was a burden. When she could no longer afford to send her older two sons to military school, she lied about their age so that John Pic could join the U.S. Coast Guard and Robert the marines. Once they were out of the house, she sent Lee Harvey to live with various relatives; by 1952 he had attended six different schools.

That year, his mother decided to move to New York City, where John Pic was stationed. Lee Harvey disliked his new home and hated his new school. He began skipping classes, and eventually his absences became so frequent that school officials declared him a habitual, uncontrollable truant. This meant that the court could take him away from his mother, but first he had to be examined by psychiatrists. They decided that Lee Harvey was emotionally disturbed and attributed his condition to the lack of affection from his mother. Moreover, they recommended that both he and Marguerite receive psychiatric treatment. Not wanting to cooperate with authorities, she fled New York before the court could act on the psychiatrists' recommendations, taking her youngest son back to New Orleans.

Lee Harvey quit school entirely after completing the ninth grade, and at age seventeen he enlisted in the U.S. Marine Corps. He performed well in his military duties, earning a sharpshooter qualification with an M-1 rifle as well as skills related to operating radio and radar equipment. He also displayed a talent for learning foreign languages, becoming fluent in Russian. But he did not fit in well with other marines and made no friends. In addi-

Oswald poses with a rifle. In the Marine Corps, he earned a sharpshooter qualification with an M-1 rifle.

tion, he increasingly got into trouble with his superior officers for arguing with them and for failing to dress properly. He was court-martialed twice, once for insulting an officer and another time for possessing an unregistered .22-caliber pistol. His punishment on both occasions was confinement and hard labor.

Life in the Soviet Union

Finally, Oswald decided he wanted out of the military. On September 11, 1959, he went to his superiors and requested a "hardship" discharge, claiming that his mother had been injured at work and could not manage without his help. The U.S. Marine Corps approved his discharge and sent him to Fort Worth, Texas, where his mother was then living.

But Oswald did not stay to help his mother. Only three days later, he traveled to New Orleans and booked passage on a ship headed to Europe. From there he went to the Soviet Union, thinking that the Soviet government would easily accept him. In a letter dated October 16, 1959, Oswald wrote,

> To the [Supreme] Soviet of the USSR, I Lee Harvey Oswald request that I be granted citizenship in the Soviet Union. . . . I want citizenship because I am a Communist and a worker. I have lived in a decadent capitalist society where the workers are slaves. I am 20 years old. I have completed three years in the United States Marine Corps. I [served] with the occupation forces in Japan, I have seen American military imperialism in all its forms.[63]

Oswald further stated that he never wanted to leave the Soviet Union, adding that he did not have enough money for his return passage to the United States anyway. He also professed his willingness to renounce his American citizenship in order to stay.

Oswald's case caught the attention of some of the Soviet Union's highest officials, who perceived him as a troubled young man. Soviet foreign minister Andrei Gromyko rejected Oswald's request because he considered the defector's state to be mentally unstable. In fact, after receiving the rejection, Oswald slit his wrists in a halfhearted suicide attempt.

Longing for Home

But although the government refused to grant Soviet citizenship to Oswald, it did allow him to remain in the country and work. He was sent to live in the city of Minsk and was given a job as a metalworker in a radio and television factory. As with most defectors, the government supplemented his salary and set him up in a good apartment. Thus, Oswald lived better than most native-born Russians.

However, at the factory he found it no easier to take orders from authority figures than he had in the past. Soon he was complaining about various aspects of Soviet life and government, and in his diary he wrote about missing American nightclubs, bowling alleys, and other places where people could have fun. He also expressed hatred for the lack of personal freedom in the Soviet Union and said he wanted to go home.

A short time later, Oswald met and married Marina Prusakova, the niece of a Communist official with whom he had become acquainted. He then began making arrangements with the U.S. embassy in Moscow to move with his wife to the United States. While they waited for approval, Marina gave birth to a daughter. Oswald borrowed money from relatives and from the U.S. government to help pay their travel expenses.

Instability

Finally, in July 1962, Oswald returned to America with his family, settling in Fort Worth. Although Oswald got a job as a metalworker, his instability continued to plague him. In October he quit his job and went to Dallas to work for a photography firm. He was fired the following April for failing to get along with his coworkers. Oswald then moved his family to New Orleans, where he found work as a greaser and oiler of coffee-processing machines. Again he was fired.

Oswald's wife, Marina (pictured), quickly embraced the materialism of the United States.

Meanwhile, his relationship with his wife was deteriorating. Oswald had expected Marina to be a dedicated Communist, rejecting the materialism prevalent in America. Instead, she badgered Oswald to buy her things and ridiculed him for his job problems and low wages. The couple fought often, and Marina usually got her way. Nonetheless, in April 1963 she left him. Four months later she gave birth to their second daughter, and the couple soon reconciled. However, their relationship remained rocky, and by November of that year they had once again separated.

Around this time, Oswald became obsessed with Cuba, which was an ally of the Soviet Union. He created a group called Fair Play for Cuba and handed out literature that favored Cuba's dictator, Fidel Castro. America's relationship with Cuba and its leader had been difficult for a couple of years, and President Kennedy's handling of the relations had been controversial. In 1961 the United States had backed an unsuccessful attempt to overthrow Castro. The following year the United States had threatened nuclear war over the Soviet Union's placement of nuclear missiles in Cuba.

Perhaps it was Kennedy's handling of Cuba that led Oswald to decide to kill the president, but those who knew him best believe otherwise. Marina later recalled, "He wanted in any way, whether good or bad, to do something that would make him outstanding, that he would be known in history."[64] Similarly, his brother Robert said that Oswald "tried to gain the world's attention through violence and destruction. . . . I am convinced that Lee

Oswald supported Cuban leader Fidel Castro (pictured) and was disturbed by President Kennedy's handling of Cuba.

could easily have chosen as his victim someone entirely different politically from John F. Kennedy."[65]

Regardless of his motive, Oswald apparently began planning the assassination in early 1963. In March he purchased a .38-caliber revolver under the name A. Hidell. He also ordered an Italian rifle with a Japanese high-powered scope. After receiving the rifle, Oswald spent several hours practicing with it.

"We're Hit!"

In October 1963 Oswald got a temporary job at the Texas School Book Depository, a seven-story building in Dallas. He had been working there for three weeks when he heard that Kennedy would be visiting Dallas and that the presidential motorcade would be passing right by the depository on the morning of November 22, 1963.

On that day, Oswald went to work at the depository as usual, carrying with him a brown paper sack that he would later claim had contained his lunch. Witnesses subsequently said it had been a two-foot-long package and reported that Oswald had told them it held a curtain rod. However, witnesses added that they believed it was too short to hold a disassembled rifle, which is what the police believed it had been used to carry and conceal.

Shortly before 12:30 P.M., the president's motorcade passed below the windows of the depository. Kennedy was sitting in a limousine with its top down, along with Texas governor John Connally, the two men's wives, and some Secret Service agents. Suddenly shots rang out. Kennedy clutched at his throat and slumped over as a Secret Service agent cried out, "We're hit!" Connally felt a bullet pierce his back and screamed out, "They're trying to kill us all!"[66] Then another bullet struck Kennedy in the head. The limousine rushed to the hospital, but doctors could not save the president's life. The governor's wounds were less serious and he eventually recovered.

Evidence Mounts

In the seconds after the shooting, a motorcycle officer who had been in the motorcade, Marion Baker, ran inside the depository, convinced that the gunfire had come from there. Inside, he met with the building manager and together the two began searching the building. They encountered Oswald in the second-floor lunchroom, where he was buying a soda, but because Oswald was an employee, they did not detain him. Instead, they continued their search, whereupon Oswald left the depository.

Forty-five minutes later he was seen entering a room he had rented. Based on witness reports, police officers concluded that Oswald had gotten there by walking seven blocks to a bus stop, taking a bus that went past the depository, leaving the bus, getting into a cab, and taking the cab to his rooming house, where he remained only briefly. By his own account, Oswald had gone there to retrieve his revolver.

Meanwhile, witnesses to the assassination reported seeing a man with a rifle in a depository window. On the building's sixth floor, officers found some boxes stacked higher than normal to conceal a window with a perfect view of the street below. Beneath that window someone had placed a shorter stack of boxes on which a gun barrel could have rested and a nearby box that could have been used as a seat. There were three empty rifle shells on the floor.

Near this site officers discovered a homemade bag whose brown wrapping paper and tape were the same as the kind used by depository employees. At first the police could not figure out what this bag might have been used for, but when they found a rifle amid another stack of cartons, they realized that the disassembled gun would have fit perfectly into the cone-shaped bag. Later, they concluded that this was the bag Oswald had been seen carrying to work that morning.

A fingerprint and palmprint matching Oswald's were on the outside of the bag, and inside was a fiber similar to those found in

A reporter looks through a gunsight from the sixth floor window of the Texas Book Depository, the same window from which Oswald shot the president.

a blanket in Oswald's home. The gun was the Italian rifle that had been sold to "A. Hidell." Experts eventually determined that this rifle had fired the bullets that killed the president and wounded Governor Connally. Moreover, a few fibers clinging to the weapon were similar to those in the shirt Oswald was wearing that day.

Oswald's Capture

However, at the time that the rifle was found, the police as yet had no clues regarding the assassin's identity. Then Officer John Tippet, who was patrolling near Oswald's rooming house, noticed a man who fit witness descriptions of the assassin and confronted him. The man shot Tippet four times with a revolver before jogging away. A bystander who witnessed this shooting used Tippet's radio to call for help.

Shortly thereafter, the manager of a nearby shoe store, Johnny Brewer, was monitoring the police radio frequency and learned about Tippet's killing. About that time he spotted a man hurrying past his store window, trying to hide his face. Suspicious, Brewer followed the stranger to a nearby theater, where the man went inside without stopping to buy a ticket. Brewer alerted the cashier, who called the police.

Brewer accompanied officers into the theater and pointed out the suspicious man. After a brief struggle, several police officers handcuffed the suspect and took him into custody. The man, later identified as Oswald, complained, "I don't know why you're doing this to me. The only thing I have done is carry a pistol in a movie."[67]

Repeated Denials

During subsequent questioning by the police, Oswald continued to insist that he had committed no crime. When police officers found two identification cards with the name A. Hidell in Oswald's wallet, one bearing Oswald's picture, he refused to acknowledge that they were his. He also denied owning a rifle, even after the police went to his house and found photographs of him holding a rifle that looked just like the one they had found at the depository. Marina Oswald told investigators that she had taken the pictures in her backyard; Oswald countered that the photographs were fakes, adding that the face was his but the body was not.

Police found the rifle used in the assassination in the Texas Book Depository (pictured). At Oswald's house they found photographs of him holding a similar rifle.

Oswald argued with the police on many other points and refused to answer some questions entirely. Meanwhile, his wife told police officers that he had been acting strangely before the assassination. She reported that the previous night he had visited her unexpectedly and spent some time in her garage before going to bed. The next morning when he went to work, he left behind his wedding ring and $170.

As Oswald continued to claim innocence, witnesses identified him as the man who had killed Officer Tippet. However, there were discrepancies in the descriptions. These witnesses recalled that Oswald had been wearing a light-colored jacket at the time, whereas someone at his rooming house recalled that he had been wearing a dark jacket. Moreover, none of the witnesses who had seen the rifleman in the depository window could positively identify Oswald as being that man, and depository employees disagreed on whether Oswald could have been on the sixth floor of the building prior to the assassination.

A Fatal Transfer

Conflicting witnesses, a lack of positive identification, and Oswald's own repeated denials cast some doubt on his guilt. Nonetheless, he was charged with both Tippet's murder and the assassination of the president, and the police decided to transfer him to the county jail on the morning of November 24. Because there had been threats against Oswald's life, police officials debated how to conduct this transfer. They finally decided to drive Oswald to the county jail in an armored truck, taking him through a basement corridor to reach the vehicle.

Oswald's transfer began shortly after 11:00 A.M. Before being led into the basement, he asked police officers for a disguise, expressing concern for his safety and complaining that the press had already reported what clothes he would be wearing. In response, a detective gave him an old black sweater. Oswald was then led toward the armored truck, past more than seventy police officers and over forty reporters. Among the spectators was Jack Ruby, a Dallas nightclub owner with ties to organized crime. Ruby was well known to the police because he made a practice of providing them with free food and drinks and attending police funerals and fund-raising events.

As Oswald was being led to the armored truck during his jail transfer, Ruby stepped from the crowd, pulled out a gun, and fired one shot directly into Oswald's abdomen. Detectives arrested Ruby while Oswald was rushed to Parkland Hospital, where he was pronounced dead at 1:07 P.M.

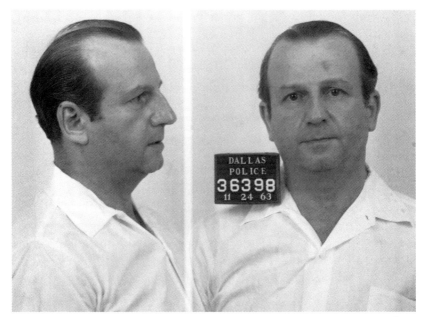

Jack Ruby (pictured), a Dallas nightclub owner who had ties to organized crime, shot and killed Oswald on November 24, 1963.

Two Funerals

Oswald's body was buried on the same day as the president's, but the circumstances of their funerals were quite different. Shortly after the president died, his body was taken to the White House for an official lying-in-state, and on November 24 his coffin was placed on a two-wheeled cart for an elaborate, televised funeral procession that would take it from the White House to the Capitol building. There, a memorial service was held, and the next day another funeral procession took the coffin to St. Matthew's Cathedral, where a huge funeral service was held. After the service the coffin was again placed on the cart, this time for a procession to Arlington National Cemetery, where the president was buried with military honors. During all of these processions and services, the nation mourned.

Meanwhile, Oswald was buried in a small, quiet funeral at Rose Hill Cemetery in Fort Worth. The only people present were Oswald's wife, Marina; his two daughters; his mother, Marguerite; and his brother, Robert. The minister who was supposed to conduct the service did not show up, so the executive secretary of the Fort Worth Area Council of Churches, Louis Saunders, agreed to say a few words. No pallbearers were present either, so some of the news reporters present agreed to carry the coffin from the chapel to the gravesite.

President Kennedy's coffin is taken to the Capitol building on November 24. The president was buried at Arlington National Cemetery the following day.

Later, Saunders said,

> There was a dim awareness in me of the tremendous contrast between the beautiful and carefully worked-out service for President Kennedy and the very humble and stark service we were having [for Oswald]. . . . The service itself probably took about ten minutes. The family left very quickly after it was over.[68]

Similarly, one of the reporters who had acted as a pallbearer recalled, "I can assure you I had no sense of history that day. It was a story and an unpleasant story at the scene of a very unpleasant news day."[69]

The Aftermath

One consequence of Kennedy's assassination was that killing the president of the United States was made a federal offense, rather than a state crime. Moreover, in the years since the murders of Kennedy and Oswald, unanswered questions regarding the circumstances of the killing have left people wondering if everyone who had a hand in the assassination has been brought to justice.

One suspicion that has lingered in the minds of some is that Oswald and Ruby were both part of a larger conspiracy. Ruby's movements on the day of the assassination are used to support this view. According to various witnesses, just before the assassination Ruby was in Dealey Plaza, and he was at Parkland Hospital when President Kennedy was being treated there for his wounds. Ruby was also at a special press conference held in the basement of police headquarters the night Oswald was arrested. When someone at the press conference said that Oswald had been a member of the Free Cuba Movement, it was Jack Ruby who corrected him by saying, "No, it's the Fair Play for Cuba Committee."[70]

Because Ruby had such a close relationship with the police, a few people suspected that the government had somehow been behind Oswald's murder. Ruby's ties with organized crime led others to believe that the Mafia had been involved with Kennedy's assassination. Still others, noting Oswald's connections to Cuba and the Soviet Union, thought that Communists had been behind the president's death. Regardless of who else they thought was involved, many people doubted that Oswald had plotted and executed the assassination by himself.

Theories that other gunmen were shooting at Kennedy from other locations have circulated ever since the day of the assassination. Although some theories seem plausible, none has been supported by hard evidence. The only physical evidence—the bullet shells and rifle found in the Texas School Book Depository—points to Lee Harvey Oswald as the assassin.

To address the public's doubts immediately following the assassination, in November 1963 the government created a special commission to determine whether Oswald had been the lone assassin or part of a conspiracy. Called the Warren Commission, in September 1964 it concluded that Oswald had acted alone, as had Jack Ruby, and that only three shots had been fired during the assassination.

In the decades following Kennedy's death, many people have refused to accept the Warren Commission's findings, and various assassination conspiracy theories have been proposed. However, many experts in the assassination personality point out that Oswald did indeed fit the common profile of an assassin. For example, FBI criminal profiler John Douglas says,

> it would make much more sense that it took a network of
> powerful, sophisticated, and evil people to change the

Two men share the shocking news of President Kennedy's assassination.

course of history, rather than one misguided [loser] who couldn't hold down a decent job. But that isn't what the evidence points to. The fact of the matter is that Oswald conforms pretty classically to the assassin profile we've come up with. He was a paranoid individual who didn't fit in with any group he tried to become part of.[71]

Oswald was the last assassin to succeed in killing an American president. He was not by any means the last person to make the attempt, however.

CHAPTER 6

The Cult Member

Although Lynette "Squeaky" Fromme pointed a gun at President Gerald Ford on September 5, 1975, she insisted that she had never intended to kill the president, and there was some evidence to support this contention. However, Fromme's history indicates that she fits the assassin personality quite well.

An Abusive Father

Born on October 22, 1948, in Santa Monica, California, Lynette Fromme grew up in the West Los Angeles area, the oldest of three children. Her mother was a housewife and her father an aerospace engineer who verbally abused his family. He treated Lynette with particular disdain. In fact, he was so much crueler to her than to her siblings that many people assumed she must be his stepdaughter.

Despite her father's abuse, Lynette was a vivacious, outgoing girl. When she was in elementary school she joined a children's dance troupe called the Lariats, which had ties to the Hollywood entertainment community, and performed at many professional venues in Los Angeles and on national television. She also went with the Lariats on cross-country tours. Lynette's time with the Lariats came to an end, however, when she and her family moved to a different part of town and her father refused to drive her to rehearsals.

Always troubled, Lynette's relationship with her father took a turn for the worse when she entered her teenage years. Shortly after she turned thirteen, he announced that she was no longer part of the family, and from then on the

President Gerald Ford (pictured) was the target of two assassination attempts.

two rarely spoke except to argue. Sometimes these arguments resulted in violence; Lynette usually wore long sleeves or long skirts to hide bruises.

To escape the abuse, Lynette often ran away from home, living with friends for days or weeks. She developed a drinking problem and became extremely depressed. She attempted suicide twice, once with an overdose of pills and another time by slitting her wrists. Although she received some psychiatric therapy, she remained troubled. Despite these problems, she managed to maintain good grades in school. She excelled in creative writing and performed in several school plays. For a brief time she had a boyfriend, but his parents discouraged the relationship because of Fromme's home life.

In 1966, the year Fromme graduated from high school, her father threw her out of the house. Fromme got a house-sitting job so she would have a temporary place to stay, then she moved into a rooming house and supported herself with a variety of low-paying jobs. Fromme's behavior during this time suggested that she was a young woman with serious emotional problems. She used drugs, including a powerful hallucinogen called LSD (lysergic acid diethylamide), and had many casual sexual relationships with older men. However, she managed to save enough money so that she could enroll in college the following year.

Soon, though, Fromme discovered that her meager savings were not enough to pay for her tuition, books, and living expenses. When her parents refused to give her any additional money, she had to drop out of college. She immediately headed for nearby Venice Beach, then a haven for men and women who embraced the drug culture. There, she met Charles Manson, whose friendship would lead Fromme ever deeper into a world of drugs and violence.

Manson's Charms

Manson spotted Fromme on a park bench the day she arrived in Venice. He listened to her problems and told her that they were only problems if she perceived them as such. He also told her that she was welcome to accompany him to San Francisco, where he was living with a woman named Mary Brunner. Fromme quickly decided to accept his offer.

Fourteen years older than Fromme, Manson had spent most of his life in jail, primarily for burglary and armed robbery. He had also run a prostitution ring for a while. Yet he was no ordinary felon. He had a charismatic appeal, particularly for women, and when he spoke he sounded more like a spiritual leader than an ex-convict.

His philosophy was loosely based on Scientology, a twentieth-century religion that emphasizes personal happiness. Someone acquainted with Manson once summarized his philosophy by saying, "He believed you could do no wrong, no bad. Everything was good. Whatever you do is what you are supposed to do; you are following your own karma."[72]

In keeping with this philosophy, Manson encouraged Fromme to do whatever she enjoyed

The beliefs of cult leader Charles Manson (pictured) appealed to Fromme.

doing, regardless of society's norms. Manson, Fromme, and Brunner soon became involved in a physical relationship, and when Manson attracted more followers, both men and women, these people too became physically involved with everyone else in the group. Manson directed his followers' behavior, calling the group "the Family."

When Manson decided to move to Los Angeles to become a musician, the entire Family went along. Eventually, they settled in the hills northwest of Los Angeles's San Fernando Valley, at the Spahn Movie Ranch. The owner of the property, George Spahn, had established it in the 1950s as a filming location for Hollywood Westerns, but by the late 1960s it had been abandoned by filmmakers. Nonetheless, Spahn continued to live on the ranch, operating a horse rental business.

Preparing for Helter Skelter

Fromme soon developed a close relationship with Spahn, who was elderly and nearly blind. She lived in his house and cooked for him while the rest of the Family lived in other buildings on the ranch and maintained the grounds. Spahn called Fromme "Squeaky" for her high voice, and the nickname stuck.

Meanwhile, the Family grew to approximately thirty-six members, including children. They lived off of Spahn's generosity, along with money from parents of Family members, items they made and sold, and illegal activities such as drug peddling and burglary. The police often visited the ranch to search for stolen property and drugs. They also shut down an unlicensed nightclub that the Family established on the property.

During this time, Manson predicted that America would soon experience a major race war pitting blacks against whites. Manson thought the blacks would win and take over the country, whereupon they would ask him for help running it. Manson looked forward to the war, which he called Helter Skelter, and decided to hasten its onset. He told his followers to commit a brutal, senseless murder and leave antiwhite slogans at the scene so that blacks would be blamed. Manson believed that Helter Skelter would begin when whites in positions of power reacted to the murders by oppressing blacks.

On the night of August 9, 1969, three Manson women and one man drove to the former estate of record producer Terry Melcher, who had recently refused to record Manson's music. There, they murdered Steven Parent, a young man who had been visiting the estate's caretaker, as well as actress Sharon Tate and Tate's unborn child; coffee heiress Abigail Folger and her boyfriend, Voytek Frykowski; and hairstylist Jay Sebring. Manson's followers left antiwhite messages at the scene as planned.

The following night Manson led his killers to another house, chosen because it was across the street from a friend of his. He

One of Manson's victims, Sharon Tate.

went inside and helped them tie up the two occupants, Leno and Rosemary LaBianca. Then he instructed his followers to kill the couple and left. After murdering the LaBiancas, the killers again wrote antiwhite slogans on walls at the crime scene.

Though Fromme had not taken part in any of this violence, she was soon involved in the aftermath. The killers were caught within months, after one of the murderers confessed, and Manson was arrested because he had orchestrated the crimes. Once he was in jail, Fromme acted as the group's spokesperson, dealt with the media, answered letters, and hired attorneys. She also tried to

Seen here being taken to trial are three women who were involved in the murders. Fromme acted as the spokesperson for Manson after he was arrested.

raise money for the Family, soliciting donations and selling recordings of Manson's music.

After Manson's trial began, Fromme sat outside on the sidewalk to call attention to his plight and profess his innocence. Manson later praised her for this:

> Lyn, the little girl who was always at the end of the line, the one who seldom made herself noticed, came right to the front with what she thought would do me some good. She and some of the other kids started spending their days on the street corner next to the jail. . . . It was Lyn's strength and devotion that engineered and kept that scene going. And the longer they stayed, the more publicity all of us and the trials received. . . . A couple of tabloid publications interviewed the girls and printed stories suggesting we weren't as callous and cold-blooded as the straight papers indicated.[73]

To get even more publicity, Fromme staged a media event in which she crawled on her hands and knees for fifteen miles. Following Manson's lead, she also carved an X into her forehead. Of his own action, Manson said, "I have X'd myself from your world. . . . I . . . stand opposed to what you do and what you have done in the past."[74] However, Fromme explained her X in a slightly different way: "It is . . . a falling cross. . . . It means that the system as it stands is falling. Your children don't want it anymore. . . . It is the fact that we are crossed out of the Establishment. We stand by ourselves apart from it."[75]

Unfailing Loyalty

Fromme's carved X was a mark of her solidarity with Manson; when the wound began to heal without leaving enough of a scar, she recarved the X again and again. Later she would also shave her head, again as an act of support for Manson.

Throughout the trial, Fromme remained Manson's most loyal follower, and after he was found guilty on January 25, 1971, she testified at his sentencing hearing. During her testimony, she tried to explain his philosophy and portray him as a spiritual and loving man. She also denied that he had any control over his followers:

> What man controls an earthquake? What man controls the rain? What man controls wars, even? How long has this earth been fighting with itself? . . . [Manson has] no power against anybody's will, let's say that. . . . Nothing against anybody's will. Each person has their own will and their individuality, and they do what they wish with it.[76]

Despite Fromme's efforts, Manson was sentenced to death and sent to a prison in San Francisco to await execution. Meanwhile, Squeaky had to deal with her own legal problems. During Manson's trial, she had been involved in a plot to keep a prosecution witness from testifying. Fromme was given ninety days in jail for her role in the plot. Her time in jail did nothing to cool her ardent support of Manson. Indeed, shortly after her release, Fromme was involved in an attempt to help one of Manson's friends break out of jail. The police believed that Fromme had driven the getaway car, and arrested her for the crime, however, there was insufficient evidence for a trial.

A Close Friend

In 1972 Fromme moved to San Francisco, where she shared an apartment with two other Manson women, one of them Sandy Good. Good became Fromme's closest friend, and together they tried to convince authorities to let them visit Manson in prison. Their requests were repeatedly denied. During this time, Fromme spent her days writing a book about the Family. She also wel-

Fromme (second from left) remained loyal to Manson, supporting him and petitioning for his release.

comed visitors that Manson sent to her apartment, many of whom were friends he had met in prison.

But although Fromme remained loyal to Manson, other Family members drifted away. Meanwhile, Fromme was still trying to win the right to visit Manson in prison. When he was moved to a prison near Sacramento, she and Good followed. Neither of the women had jobs; Good lived off income from a trust fund while Fromme received welfare checks and food stamps. To gain additional funds, Fromme became intimate with a much older man, Harold "Manny" Boro, who not only gave her cash but also bought her a car.

A New Religion

In prison Manson developed a new religion, which he ordered his disciples to practice. He sent Fromme letters in which he outlined some of the requirements, including prohibitions against eating meat, wearing makeup, and consorting with men. Only Fromme and Good obeyed Manson's wishes, becoming self-professed nuns in the new faith. In 1975, to set themselves apart from others, Fromme and Good began wearing red robes. Fromme explained their significance to reporters:

> We're waiting for our Lord [Manson] and there's only one thing to do before He comes off the cross and that's clean up the earth. . . . We're nuns now. . . . Our red robes are

an example of the new morality. . . . They're red with the sacrifice, the blood of the sacrifice.[77]

Cleaning up the earth soon became Fromme's obsession. She promoted environmentalism at every opportunity; at one point, she even suggested to an admirer that he could win her affection by killing the head of a corporation that Fromme believed was responsible for pollution. In a biography of Fromme, reporter Jess Brevin explains that this obsession was related to Fromme's experiences with the Family:

> Lyn had become a Manson nun. In her red robes and daily obeissances, she lived her life in ascetic devotion to the long-gone days of Spahn Ranch and Death Valley. To Lyn, there was no irony. Spahn Ranch may well have been filled with sex, drugs, and wanton irresponsibility—a focus on Now—but in retrospect, it had been about so much more. The Family had lived as a model, and eventually a warning, to the world. A warning, she decided, about the state of the ecology, about the environmental, and thus spiritual, pollution of the earth. That was what the Tate-LaBianca murders must have been about. . . . The time had come for Lyn to [commit a similar act]: Do something, like the Tate murders years before, that would capture the imagination of the world.[78]

The Court of Retribution

Once more, Fromme felt she needed to show her solidarity with Manson. This time she chose an environmental message; she and Good decided to wage war against corporate polluters. They created a fictitious two-thousand-member group called the International People's Court of Retribution and sent threatening letters in the name of the group to various corporate leaders. They told the press that the group would soon rise up to destroy major polluters everywhere.

Fromme also told friends that she was disgusted with the way President Gerald Ford was running the country, particularly in regard to environmental issues. Around this time, she obtained an antique Colt .45 revolver from Boro, telling him that she needed it for protection. Later one of Fromme's friends would say that she had wanted it to kill polluters.

At the end of the summer of 1975, Fromme heard that President Ford would be visiting her city as part of a campaign tour in California. His complete schedule was published in Sacramento newspapers, so she knew that on September 5, 1975, Ford would

After Fromme pulled out her gun, she was immediately disarmed and wrestled to the ground by Secret Service agents.

leave the Senator Hotel at 9:55 A.M. to walk across the street to the State Capitol building and meet with California's governor. As he walked, he would shake hands with spectators.

When Ford emerged from his hotel, Fromme was ready for him. She wore her long red robe and had strapped the Colt .45 to her leg. As the president moved closer, shaking hands in the crowd, Fromme pulled out the gun and aimed. What happened next is the subject of disagreement, but what is known is that within seconds a Secret Service agent, Larry Buendorf, grabbed the weapon and wrestled Fromme to the ground, aided by a policeman and a spectator.

Building a Case

After her arrest, Fromme was taken to police headquarters and given a barrage of tests that showed she was both sane and sober. In her apartment, investigators found some of her threatening letters to corporate leaders. They believed that, in her anger over the state of the environment, Fromme had intended to kill Ford. However, Fromme insisted that she had only pointed the gun at the president in order to get publicity for her environmental cause; investigators later discovered that there was no bullet in the gun's chamber, although there were bullets in the cylinder. Fromme also said that when she saw Ford, he had reminded her of her father, and she therefore had been unable to kill him.

But even Fromme's defense attorney recognized a problem with her story. If all she had wanted to do was get publicity, why had she loaded the gun at all? And if she had not gone to the event intending to kill Ford, then how could she have changed her mind about killing him when she recalled her father? Moreover, some witnesses claimed that they had heard a "click" just before the Secret Service agent grabbed Fromme's gun, meaning that she had indeed pulled the trigger. Other witnesses reported that after pulling the trigger, she had complained about the gun not going off. Fromme's trial would be a battle over intent, with both sides addressing the question of whether Fromme really had intended to kill the president.

Despite the difficulties of handling such a case, Fromme decided to act as her own attorney. She handled the jury selection process well, carefully eliminating any potential juror who was or ever had been a hunter because she felt that such a person would be prejudiced against her environmental views. She also eliminated anyone who expressed disapproval of the Manson Family. During this period, her decisions and courtroom behavior convinced the judge, Thomas MacBride, that Fromme was at least minimally competent to handle her own defense.

His opinion changed just before the start of the trial. During a procedural discussion after the jury was picked, Fromme insisted that Charles Manson be allowed to testify on her behalf as a character witness, even though she had not seen him in over six years. At first she told MacBride that Manson was the only one who knew her well enough to swear she was nonviolent. Then she changed her story, saying that she wanted him to testify so that he could share his philosophy with the American public and explain why he had been involved in the Tate-LaBianca murders.

MacBride reminded Fromme that she was the one on trial, not Manson. Nonetheless, she continued to insist that Manson be allowed to speak. When MacBride refused her request, Fromme grew angry. She tried to change her plea to guilty, saying there was no point in going to trial without Manson. At the same time, she refused to admit that she had intended to kill President Ford, which meant that MacBride could not accept her guilty plea.

The dispute with the judge grew so heated the he finally had Fromme removed from the courtroom. When he later allowed her to come back, she continued to act up, even in the presence of jurors. MacBride therefore decided that Fromme would have to watch the trial from her cell via a television monitor. In her absence, a qualified attorney handled her defense.

Guilty as Charged

Once the trial resumed, Fromme's attorney stressed that his client was experienced with firearms and therefore would have known there was no bullet in her gun's chamber. To him, this constituted proof that Fromme had never actually intended to shoot the president. One witness to the attempted assassination support-

Fromme's demand that Charles Manson be allowed to testify on her behalf was denied.

ed this contention, testifying that while Fromme was being wrestled to the ground she had said that the gun was not loaded. Prosecutors had tried to keep this witness's statement from Fromme's attorney, an act that almost led MacBride to declare a mistrial. However, the witness subsequently expressed doubts about what he had heard, and other witnesses offered contradictory reports of what Fromme said during the event.

To show that Fromme had intended to harm Ford, prosecutors presented testimony that she had tried to borrow a more reliable and compact gun prior to the assassination attempt. They also offered witnesses who heard her say she would have to kill people in order to make a statement about the environment. The prosecution's case was strong, and on November 26, 1975, the jury found Fromme guilty of attempted assassination.

Fromme had refused to testify on her own behalf, but when she went before the judge for sentencing, she once again tried to argue her point of view. He reminded her that the time for explanation was past. Then, while the prosecutor was saying that Fromme had a violent nature, she pulled an apple from beneath her robe and threw it at him, striking him in the head. She also told MacBride that she would never change her views and never be rehabilitated. In response, the judge declared her a menace to society and sentenced her to life in prison.

The Aftermath

Fromme's attempt to assassinate President Ford led the American public to demand that their presidents receive more protection. Ford approved an increase in funding for the Secret Service, and after more attempts were made on Ford's life by other would-be assassins, the government made changes in Secret Service procedures as well. These changes, however, were not enough to prevent other assassination attempts. In fact, Ford's staunch refusal to take the threat of assassination seriously and to lessen his contact with the public set a standard that might have put subsequent presidents more at risk.

CHAPTER 7

The Love-Struck Assassin

One assassination attempt that came close to succeeding was the one in which John Warnock Hinckley Jr. shot President Ronald Reagan on March 30, 1981. Dogged by a history of mental illness, Hinckley attacked Reagan in order to impress a famous actress he had never met. The president survived his wounds, but the incident triggered a national controversy regarding whether insanity should entitle someone to escape a jail sentence.

A Withdrawn Child

Born on May 29, 1955, in Ardmore, Oklahoma, John Hinckley Jr. was the youngest of three children. His older brother and sister were high achievers in school, and his father, Jack, was a successful petroleum engineer who founded his own oil company. In contrast, Hinckley's mother, Jo Anne, was a shy housewife who had difficulty making decisions. After the family moved from Ardmore to Dallas in 1958, Jo Anne developed agoraphobia, experiencing panic attacks whenever she left the house. She eventually overcame her illness but remained overprotective of her youngest son.

Partly because of his mother's protectiveness, young John rarely left his mother's side, and he had no real friends. For a brief time he was involved in school sports, but for most of his childhood he was inactive and overweight. He also rarely displayed any energy or excitement, seeming passive and quiet. His father later said, "It was always hard to tell how John felt. He didn't express emotions."[79]

Hinckley became even more isolated from his peers after he reached high school. He spent much of his time alone in his room, plucking a guitar. He told his parents that he wanted to be a rock musician and songwriter, but he could not read music and was too shy to perform in front of anyone, even his family. Therefore, his father insisted that he go to college and get a degree in business administration. Hinckley expressed some opposition to this plan, but in the end he gave in and did what his father told him to do.

Troubles in College

In 1973 Hinckley enrolled at Texas Tech University in Lubbock. He did poorly there from the outset. While living in the college dormitory, he alienated one roommate after another by being sullen and disagreeable. He also failed to complete class assignments; rather than fail courses outright, he withdrew from them without credit. At the end of the school year, he decided to quit college altogether and took a job in a Dallas pizza parlor.

By this time Hinckley's parents had moved to Denver, and they made him pay for his own apartment since he was no longer in school or living at home. Hinckley soon found

Secret Service agents escort John Hinckley Jr. (center) after his arrest.

that life was not easy, especially on his meager income. He decided to return to college so that his parents would again pay his expenses. He reenrolled at Texas Tech in early 1975, but his grades remained poor and he continued to withdraw from courses before completing them. In April 1976 he once more decided to drop out.

This time he left for Hollywood, determined to pursue his original goal of becoming a rock musician. A letter he wrote to his parents suggested that he was trying to get his life on track:

> I am trying to sell some of my songs. I've got two appointments next week to see music publishers. I've also met a guy who wants to start a group with me. But with my limited funds, I don't know if I'll be able to or not. . . . I hope you're not disappointed with me for dropping out of school so suddenly without any notice or anything. I *do* feel bad about being so inconsiderate. But one thing which is very important to me is the fact that for the first time in years I am happy.[80]

By June his circumstances had changed, and not for the better. He wrote his parents again, asking for help:

For the past 2 ½ weeks I have literally been without food, shelter, and clothing. On May 14, someone broke into my room and stole almost all of my possessions. . . . At night I have to sleep on picnic benches and the ground. . . . [I have had to] walk up to strangers and ask them for spare change, so I can eat. . . . [Nonetheless,] I honestly feel that I could achieve success here, if I only had half a chance. . . . I'm now 21 and I believe that these next few months and year will be the most crucial in my life. You don't know how grateful I would be if you could give me limited financial support and a great deal of moral support during this critical period.[81]

Highs and Lows

Hinckley's parents sent him money, and he remained in Los Angeles. His letters home were soon filled with descriptions of meetings with record producers and of his new girlfriend, an actress named Lynn Collins. Then Hinckley wrote that he had broken up with Collins and that the music industry had lost interest in his work. Shortly thereafter he flew to Denver and moved in with his parents.

Hinckley got a job as a busboy at a nightclub, but in March 1977 he abruptly flew back to California, insisting he would stay there permanently. Despite these assertions, he was back in Denver within two weeks. Although he offered little explanation for his actions, his parents paid for everything, including his airfare and tuition when he reenrolled at Texas Tech that fall.

But just as before, Hinckley did poorly at his studies and failed to make friends. By this time he had also become a hypochondriac, convinced that he had a variety of serious ailments. He went to several doctors, but no one could find anything wrong with him. He insisted that he needed a brain X ray, but the doctors refused to perform one.

Meanwhile, he wrote his parents that he had resumed his relationship with Lynn Collins and that she had encouraged him to write a novel. In December he said he could not come home for Christmas because he and Collins were going to New York, where he would show his manuscript to publishers. His subsequent letters offered glowing reports of his meetings with an agent and his experiences with Collins. After his return to school from winter vacation, he also wrote about a mailing list business that he and a friend had established. His parents sent him money to help fund the business.

In reality, there was no business. There was also no book manuscript and no Lynn Collins. Hinckley had spent Christmas alone in his Lubbock, Texas, apartment. All of what he had written in his letters had been lies; unbeknownst to his family, he still had no friends, and his weight had risen to 230 pounds on a 5-foot 10-inch frame. He was also taking Valium, which a psychiatrist he had seen had prescribed for depression.

Taxi Driver

Also unbeknownst to his family, Hinckley had become obsessed with the 1976 movie *Taxi Driver*. The main character in the movie, a New York cab driver named Travis Bickle, becomes obsessed with a woman who, in turn, is enamored with the presidential candidate upon whose campaign she is working. When the woman rejects Bickle, he stalks the candidate and almost shoots the man. Bickle continues to fantasize about his relationship with the campaign worker, writing letters to his parents in which he describes her as his girlfriend. As the film's plot develops, Bickle encounters a young prostitute, Iris; in a violent gun battle, he rescues her from the men who have ruined her life. In the end Bickle is depicted as a hero.

Hinckley strongly identified with Bickle. He wore the same clothes and ate the same food as the character; "Lynn Collins" was modeled after the campaign worker in the movie. He also

Hinckley was obsessed with the movie Taxi Driver. He wore the same clothes and ate the same food as his favorite character in the film, Travis Bickle (pictured).

bought handguns just like Bickle's and practiced with them at a rifle range, as Bickle had. In an even more ominous imitation, by October 1980 Hinckley was stalking President Jimmy Carter, then a candidate for reelection. Hinckley went to one of Carter's campaign speeches in Dayton, Ohio, and another in Nashville, Tennessee, where he was arrested for trying to take three handguns onto an airplane. Released after convincing authorities that he was harmless, he concealed the episode from his family.

While Hinckley was pursuing one fantasy, he was deceiving his parents with another. Hinckley's parents thought he was attending a writing program at Yale University in New Haven, Connecticut; they had given him over two thousand dollars for his tuition and expenses. In actuality, there was no workshop. However, Hinckley did visit Yale to stalk a student there: Jodie Foster, the actress who had played the role of Iris in *Taxi Driver*.

When Hinckley found Foster's dorm room, he slipped notes under her door. The first of these sounded like typical fan mail, but the later ones were more ominous. One of them said: "After tonight John Lennon [who had recently been murdered] and I will have a lot in common. It's all for you, Foster."[82] Another read "Jodie Foster, love, just wait. I will rescue you very soon. Please cooperate."[83] This note was similar to one that Bickle sent to Iris in *Taxi Driver*.

Hinckley stalked Jodie Foster (pictured) and sent her ominous notes.

Erratic Behavior

In early 1981 Hinckley announced that he had dropped out of the writing program at Yale and then returned home to live with his parents. Weary of their son's inability to become productive, they began taking him to a psychiatrist named John Hopper. After a few sessions, Hopper concluded that Hinckley's problems were the result of being coddled too much at home.

Hopper outlined steps whereby Hinckley would gradually become more responsible for his own actions. Although Hinckley's father was convinced that this was the right treatment, the rest of his family did not share this opinion. Hinckley's brother, sister, and brother-in-law believed that he belonged in a mental institution. His mother believed that he only needed more sympathy.

Despite the sessions with the psychiatrist, Hinckley's appearance and behavior deteriorated. His parents suspected that he had a drug problem, but his psychiatrist argued that he just needed to become responsible for himself. Hopper convinced Hinckley's parents to kick him out of their house. In response, they told Hinckley that he had to be in his own apartment by the end of March 1981.

On March 1, Hinckley disappeared for several days, then called his parents from New York City saying he wanted to fly home. He was nearly incoherent and said he had not eaten anything for a long time. His parents sent him airfare, but when he arrived at the Denver airport, his father told him that he could not come home, gave him two hundred dollars, and told him to stay at the YMCA.

Within a few days Hinckley had flown back to California, where he took a cross-country bus to Washington, D.C. He funded his travels by selling some gold coins he had stolen from his father. Once he was back in Washington, D.C., Hinckley checked into the Park Central Hotel; he learned that Ronald Reagan would be at the Hilton Hotel the next day to give a speech to a labor union council.

In his hotel room, Hinckley wrote a lengthy note to Foster in which he indicated that he was planning an attempt on Reagan's life:

> There is a definite possibility that I will be killed in my attempt to get Reagan. . . . As you well know by now, I love you very much. The past seven months I have left you dozens of poems, letters and messages in the faint hope you would develop an interest in me. . . . Jodie, I would abandon this idea of getting Reagan in a second if I could only win your heart and live out the rest of my life with you, whether it be in total obscurity or whatever. I will admit to you that the reason I'm going ahead with this attempt now is because I just cannot wait any longer to impress you. I've got to do something now to make you understand in no uncertain terms that I am doing all of this for your sake. By sacrificing my freedom and possibly my life I hope to change your mind about me. . . . Jodie, I'm asking you to please look into your heart and at least give me the chance with this historical deed to gain your respect and love.[84]

He also wrote a postcard addressed to Foster, saying, "Dear Jodie . . . one day you and I will occupy the White House and the peasants will drool with envy."[85] Then he left for the Hilton, leaving behind both the note and the postcard as well as a cassette tape, recorded on New Year's Eve, on which he said, "Anything that I might do in 1981 would be solely for Jodie Foster's sake. I want to tell the world in some way that I worship and idolize her."[86] Also left behind was a note indicating that at one point he had planned to hijack an airplane; later Hinckley would tell authorities that he had considered crashing a plane into the White House.

In a letter, Hinckley informed Foster that he was going to assassinate President Reagan (pictured) in order to impress her.

The Assassination Attempt

On the afternoon of March 30, 1981, Hinckley joined a crowd of onlookers outside of the Hilton Hotel. He had a .22-caliber short-barreled revolver loaded with a special kind of bullet called a Devastator, which was designed to do maximum damage by exploding on impact. He watched as Reagan exited the hotel at approximately 2:25 P.M., accompanied by his press secretary, James Brady; senior aide Michael Deaver; a physician; and some Secret Service agents and police officers. Then, as the group walked toward a waiting limousine and Reagan waved to the crowd, Hinckley fired six shots at him in less than two seconds.

According to a government reconstruction of the event based on ballistics, the first bullet struck James Brady in the head. The second hit a District of Columbia police officer, Thomas K. Delahanty, in the neck. The third went into a building across the street. The fourth hit Secret Service agent Timothy J. McCarthy in the chest. The fifth hit the limousine's window. The sixth shot struck the limousine, then ricocheted and hit Reagan in the chest under the left arm.

Immediately after he had discharged his weapon, Hinckley was tackled by Secret Service agents. Meanwhile, the wounded were rushed to the hospital. They were all in critical condition, although reports at the time minimized the seriousness of the presi-

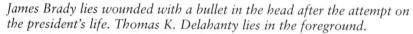

James Brady lies wounded with a bullet in the head after the attempt on the president's life. Thomas K. Delahanty lies in the foreground.

dent's injury. The person in the most serious condition was James Brady, who barely survived and suffered permanent brain damage.

Mental Problems Worsen

Under arrest, Hinckley was kept in a series of facilities where he was subjected to psychiatric tests, head X rays, and brain scans. During this time he tried to commit suicide, hoarding medication until he had enough for an overdose. Before the pills could kill him, however, he was discovered and treated by doctors.

Hinckley was now kept confined under constant surveillance. Restless, bored, and impatient for his trial to begin, Hinckley fabricated a conspiracy, writing notes detailing his participation in a plot to kill the president. The FBI took these notes seriously, and Hinckley's trial was delayed as investigators checked out the validity of his story. In the end, FBI agents determined that Hinckley's conspiracy was just another of his fantasies.

Hinckley had also written to the news media, demanding attention from Jodie Foster. His writings were so blatantly disturbed that many who read them thought he must be faking insanity in order to build a defense on that basis. Even after a second unsuccessful suicide attempt, the public refused to believe he was really insane.

The Jury's Verdict

Finally, on April 27, 1982, Hinckley's trial began. He had been charged with assaulting and attempting to kill President Reagan, James Brady, Thomas K. Delahanty, and Timothy J. McCarthy, both as individuals and as federal officials. For much of the trial, however, experts for each side argued over Hinckley's sanity. Defense attorneys did not dispute the contention that Hinckley had committed the shooting, but they argued that he was not sane at the time. Three psychiatrists testifying for the defense supported this assessment. In addition, doctors presented evidence that Hinckley's brain exhibited slight physical abnormalities, although they offered no proof that such abnormalities were an indication of psychological illness.

Psychiatrists for the prosecution, however, argued that Hinckley met the legal definition of sanity during the assassination attempt because he knew at the time that his act was wrong. They suggested that Hinckley wanted fame but was neither hardworking nor talented enough to achieve it. Therefore, they argued, he had decided to commit a crime guaranteed to bring him the most attention. One prosecution psychiatrist added that, in his opinion,

Hinckley was clearly faking insanity in order to be found not guilty.

The trial lasted eight weeks. Five days after it ended, the jury reached a verdict: not guilty by reason of insanity on all charges. Expecting and hoping for a guilty verdict, many members of the public were outraged. What particularly outraged some was the prospect that Hinckley could be released into society whenever his own psychiatrists declared him sane and a court agreed with this assessment. However, his attorneys stated that they would not work toward his release, and his parents issued a statement saying that he would be confined at St. Elizabeth's Mental Hospital in Washington, D.C., until there was absolutely no doubt that he was harmless.

But Hinckley himself taunted the public, reminding them that his not guilty verdict meant that he would indeed go free some-day. He also wrote a letter to the *New York Times* in which he said,

> The shooting outside the Washington Hilton hotel was the greatest love offering in the history of the world. I sacrificed myself and committed the ultimate crime in hopes of winning the heart of a girl. It was an unprecedented demonstration of love. But does the American public appreciate what I've done? Does Jodie Foster appreciate what I've done?[87]

Fighting for Release

At St. Elizabeth's Mental Hospital, Hinckley continued to be obsessed with Foster, secretly collecting photographs of her. The doctors there judged Hinckley to have a form of mental illness known as schizophrenia, and he was told he would have to remain in the hospital indefinitely. This led Hinckley to attempt suicide once again. However, as years passed he turned his attention toward fighting for his own release. He petitioned the court on several occasions to let him out of the hospital, claiming that he was cured. Eventually his doctors agreed with this assessment and supported his petitions.

Hinckley seemed to take pride in having somehow deceived his doctors. As Hinckley himself wrote in his diary in 1987,

> I dare say that not one psychiatrist who has analyzed me knows any more about me than the average person on the street who has read about me in the newspapers. Psychiatry is a guessing game and I do my best to keep the fools

guessing about me. They will never know the true John Hinckley. Only I fully understand myself.[88]

In fact, during one period when St. Elizabeth's doctors were expressing their support for Hinckley's release, it was discovered that Hinckley had been writing to two imprisoned murderers, Charles Manson and Ted Bundy. He had also substituted his obsession with Foster for an obsession with a pharmacist at the hospital, Jeannette Wick. After learning these facts, hospital physicians withdrew their support for release, and the court rejected Hinckley's petition.

While in St. Elizabeth Hospital, Hinckley wrote to serial murderer Ted Bundy (pictured).

Nonetheless, Hinckley continued fighting for his freedom. After several lawsuits, a federal appeals court ruled that Hinckley's doctors, rather than a court, had the exclusive power to determine whether Hinckley was sane enough to be released. In August 1999 the hospital's doctors pronounced Hinckley cured and started planning supervised outings for their patient in preparation for his eventual release.

In the months following this announcement, public debate about whether Hinckley had been cured and about whether he was ever really insane to begin with continued. Several psychiatrists spoke out against St. Elizabeth's decision, saying that schizophrenia recurs unless a patient continues to take the proper medication. Therefore, one of the foremost authorities on schizophrenia, E. Fuller Torrey, has said that it would be "unfair to the people in this community and unfair to Jodie Foster to release him unless he is on medication."[89] Hinckley has taken no such medication since 1992.

But officials at St. Elizabeth's countered that Hinckley was ready to lead a normal life. As proof, they pointed to his engagement to Leslie deVeau, whom he met while she was also a patient at St. Elizabeth's; deVeau killed her ten-year-old daughter with a shotgun in 1982, but the hospital pronounced her cured of insanity in 1985.

Like Hinckley, deVeau had successfully pleaded not guilty by reason of insanity.

The Aftermath

Immediately after Hinckley's trial, several laws were proposed to end or severely curtail the use of the insanity defense. For example, Reagan's attorney general, William French Smith, went before Congress to argue that mental illness should only be a defense for someone who did not even know he had a gun in his hand or that he was shooting at a person. Meanwhile, President Reagan suggested that the law be changed to substitute the not-guilty-by-reason-of-insanity verdict with "guilty but insane."

After Hinckley's trial, Attorney General William French Smith fought to limit the use of the insanity defense.

Over a dozen states have since adopted the guilty-but-insane option for juries trying to reach a verdict. In addition, slight changes were made at the federal level to make it more difficult for a defendant to plead not guilty by reason of insanity. For example, the burden of proof is now on the defense rather than the prosecution, which means that the prosecution no longer has to prove that the defendant is sane in order to win a conviction. Instead, the defense must prove the defendant's insanity.

The controversy over the use of the insanity defense has yet to be resolved. Also yet to be resolved is the problem of how presidents can be protected from disturbed individuals while continuing to respect the freedoms that presidents swear to uphold.

NOTES

Introduction: A Unique Type of Murder

1. Gerald R. Ford, *A Time to Heal: The Autobiography of Gerald R. Ford*. New York: Harper & Row and Reader's Digest, 1979, p. 310.

2. Quoted in Lance Gay, "Notorious Assassins Cut from Same Disaffected Cloth," Scripts News Service, July 29, 1998.

Chapter 1: Political and Personal Causes

3. James McKinley, *Assassination in America*. New York: Harper & Row, 1977, p. xi.

4. Albert Ellis and John M. Gullo, *Murder and Assassination*. New York: Lyle Stuart, 1971, pp. 192–93.

5. Ellis and Gullo, *Murder and Assassination*, p. 250.

6. John Douglas and Mark Olshaker, *The Anatomy of Motive*. New York: Lisa Drew Book/Scribners, 1999, p. 239.

7. Ellis and Gullo, *Murder and Assassination*, p. 198.

8. Douglas and Olshaker, *The Anatomy of Motive*, p. 238.

9. McKinley, *Assassination in America*, p. xii.

10. Douglas and Olshaker, *The Anatomy of Motive*, p. 235.

11. Ellis and Gullo, *Murder and Assassination*, p. 209.

12. Quoted in Ellis and Gullo, *Murder and Assassination*, p. 249.

13. McKinley, *Assassination in America*, p. 3.

14. Ellis and Gullo, *Murder and Assassination*, p. 199.

15. Ellis and Gullo, *Murder and Assassination*, pp. 190–91.

16. McKinley, *Assassination in America*, p. 223.

17. Ford, *A Time to Heal*, p. 312.

18. McKinley, *Assassination in America*, p. 223.

19. McKinley, *Assassination in America*, p. 224.

20. Mimi Hall, "White House Visit Is No Magic Carpet Ride," *USA Today*, February 5, 1998, p. 10A.

Chapter 2: The Southern Sympathizer

21. Eleanor Ruggles, *Prince of Players: Edwin Booth*. New York: W. W. Norton, 1953, p. 164.

22. Jim Bishop, *The Day Lincoln Was Shot*, New York: Harper & Row, 1955, p. 62.

23. Bishop, *The Day Lincoln Was Shot*, p. 62.

24. Ruggles, *Prince of Players*, p. 119.

25. Ruggles, *Prince of Players*, p. 178.

26. Quoted in Ruggles, *Prince of Players*, p. 178.

27. Quoted in Ruggles, *Prince of Players*, p. 178.

28. Ellis and Gullo, *Murder and Assassination*, p. 233.

29. Bishop, *The Day Lincoln Was Shot*, p. 63.

30. Quoted in Bishop, *The Day Lincoln Was Shot*, pp. 71–72.

31. Quoted in Ruggles, *Prince of Players*, p. 179.

32. Quoted in Bishop, *The Day Lincoln Was Shot*, p. 209.

33. Quoted in Bishop, *The Day Lincoln Was Shot*, p. 209.

34. Quoted in Ruggles, *Prince of Players*, p. 186.

35. McKinley, *Assassination in America*, pp. 29–30.

36. McKinley, *Assassination in America*, p. 33.

37. McKinley, *Assassination in America*, p. 39.

Chapter 3: A Disgruntled Office Seeker

38. Quoted in James C. Clark, *The Murder of James A. Garfield*. Jefferson, NC: McFarland, 1993, pp. 5–6.

39. Quoted in Clark, *The Murder of James A. Garfield*, p. 7.

40. Quoted in Clark, *The Murder of James A. Garfield*, p. 21.

41. Quoted in McKinley, *Assassination in America*, p. 45.

42. Quoted in McKinley, *Assassination in America*, p. 47.

43. Quoted in McKinley, *Assassination in America*, p. 46.

44. Quoted in McKinley, *Assassination in America*, p. 46.

45. Quoted in McKinley, *Assassination in America*, p. 48.

46. Quoted in Ellis and Gullo, *Murder and Assassination*, p. 235.

47. Quoted in Ellis and Gullo, *Murder and Assassination*, p. 235.

48. Quoted in McKinley, *Assassination in America*, p. 49.

49. Justus D. Doenecke, *The Presidencies of James A. Garfield and Chester A. Arthur*. Lawrence: Regents Press of Kansas, 1981, pp. 95–96.

50. McKinley, *Assassination in America*, p. 50.

51. Quoted in Thomas C. Reeves, *Gentleman Boss: The Life of Chester Alan Arthur.* New York: Knopf, 1975, p. 264.

52. Charles E. Rosenberg, *The Trial of the Assassin Guiteau: Psychiatry and Law in the Gilded Age.* Chicago: University of Chicago Press, 1968, p. 237.

Chapter 4: The Anarchist

53. Liz A. Highleyman, "An Introduction to Anarchism," p. 1. www.etext.org/Politics/Spunk/library/intro/sp001550.html.

54. Margaret Leech, *In the Days of McKinley.* New York: Harper & Brothers, 1959, p. 561.

55. Leech, *In the Days of McKinley,* pp. 561–62.

56. Quoted in Pan-American Exposition, "Secret Service Guard Ireland Tells Story of Anarchist's Deed." http://intotem.buffnet.net/bhw/panamex/assassination/article5.htm.

57. Quoted in Leech, *In the Days of McKinley,* p. 595.

58. Quoted in McKinley, *Assassination in America,* p. 56.

59. Quoted in McKinley, *Assassination in America,* p. 56.

60. Quoted in McKinley, *Assassination in America,* p. 56.

61. McKinley, *Assassination in America,* p. 57.

62. McKinley, *Assassination in America,* p. 56.

Chapter 5: The Lone Gunman—or Conspirator?

63. Quoted in David Hoffman, "Oswald Letter Is Among Documents from Russia," *Washington Post,* June 23, 1999, p. A15.

64. Quoted in Ellis and Gullo, *Murder and Assassination,* p. 217.

65. Quoted in Ellis and Gullo, *Murder and Assassination,* p. 217.

66. Quoted in Jim Bishop, *The Day Kennedy Was Shot.* New York: Funk & Wagnalls, 1968, p. 175.

67. Quoted in Bishop, *The Day Kennedy Was Shot,* p. 278.

68. Dallas Morning News, *November 22: The Day Remembered as Reported by the Dallas Morning News.* Dallas: Taylor, 1990, p. 116.

69. Dallas Morning News, *November 22,* p. 166.

70. Quoted in Dallas Morning News, *November 22,* p. 54.

71. Douglas and Olshaker, *The Anatomy of Motive,* p. 249.

Chapter 6: The Cult Member

72. Vincent Bugliosi with Curt Gentry, *Helter Skelter.* New York: Bantam, 1995, p. 300.

73. Charles Manson, as told to Nuel Emmons, *Manson in His Own Words*. New York: Grove, 1986, p. 223.

74. Quoted in Bugliosi, *Helter Skelter*, p. 421.

75. Quoted in Jess Brevin, *Squeaky: The Life and Times of Lynette Fromme*. New York: St. Martin's Griffin, 1997, p. 138.

76. Quoted in Brevin, *Squeaky*, p. 136.

77. Quoted in Brevin, *Squeaky*, p. 191.

78. Brevin, *Squeaky*, p. 193.

Chapter 7: The Love-Struck Assassin

79. Jack and Jo Anne Hinckley, *Breaking Points*. Grand Rapids, MI: Chosen Books (Zondervan), 1985, p. 70.

80. Quoted in Hinckley, *Breaking Points*, p. 84.

81. Quoted in Hinckley, *Breaking Points*, pp. 86–87.

82. Quoted in Hinckley, *Breaking Points*, pp. 297–98.

83. Quoted in Hinckley, *Breaking Points*, p. 298.

84. Quoted in Hinckley, *Breaking Points*, p. 169.

85. Quoted in Hinckley, *Breaking Points*, p. 282.

86. Quoted in Hinckley, *Breaking Points*, p. 171.

87. Quoted in Hinckley, *Breaking Points*, p. 341.

88. Quoted in Mike Feinsilber, "Hinckley, Still 'Dangerous,' Loses Bid for Occasional Freedom," Associated Press, April 15, 1998.

89. Quoted in Mary Leonard, "The Hinckley Debate: Doctors Say Reagan's Shooter Healthy Enough to Leave Hospital, but Some Wonder if He's Deceiving Them," *Dallas Morning News*, August 7, 1999, p. 16A.

FOR FURTHER READING

Books

Bill G. Cox, et al., *Crimes of the Twentieth Century*. New York: Crescent Books, 1991. This book offers information and photographs related to Lee Harvey Oswald, Charles Manson and his "Family," and John W. Hinckley Jr.

Wilborn Hampton, *Kennedy Assassinated! The World Mourns: A Reporter's Story*. Cambridge, MA: Candlewick, 1997. Written by a Dallas reporter who was working when President John F. Kennedy was assassinated, this book for young adults gives a minute-by-minute account, with photographs, of what happened that day.

Rebecca C. Jones, *The President Has Been Shot: True Stories of the Attacks on Ten U.S. Presidents*. New York: Dutton Books, 1996. This young adult book discusses the assassinations of four American presidents and the attempted assassinations of six others; it also includes a wide variety of conspiracy theories related to these events.

Jo Anne Ray, *American Assassins*. Minneapolis: Lerner, 1974. This book for young adults offers information about assassins who have killed prominent Americans, including presidents.

Stephen Sondheim and John Weidman, *Assassins*. New York: Theatre Communications Group, 1991. This book provides the lyrics of the Stephen Sondheim musical *Assassins*, which presents the lives and motivations of America's presidential assassins.

Time-Life Books, *Assassination*. Alexandria, VA: Time-Life Books, 1992. Part of a series on notorious crimes, this book discusses assassination and offers biographical information on famous assassins throughout history.

Karen Zeinert, *The Lincoln Murder Plot*. North Haven, CT: Linnet Books, 1999. This young adult book offers information about the assassination of President Abraham Lincoln.

WORKS CONSULTED

Books

Herbert Abrams, *The President Has Been Shot: Confusion, Disability, and the Twenty-fifth Amendment in the Aftermath of the Attempted Assassination of Ronald Reagan.* New York: W. W. Norton, 1992. Written by a physician, this book discusses John W. Hinckley's attempt to assassinate President Ronald Reagan and criticizes the way the crisis was managed while Reagan was in the hospital.

Jim Bishop, *The Day Kennedy Was Shot.* New York: Funk & Wagnalls, 1968. This book offers a minute-by-minute account of the day President John F. Kennedy was shot.

————, *The Day Lincoln Was Shot.* New York: Harper & Row, 1955. This book also offers a minute-by-minute account of the day President Abraham Lincoln was shot.

Jess Brevin, *Squeaky: The Life and Times of Lynette Fromme.* New York: St. Martin's Griffin, 1997. Reporter Jess Brevin provides a highly detailed biography of Lynette Fromme, who attempted to assassinate President Gerald Ford.

Vincent Bugliosi with Curt Gentry, *Helter Skelter.* New York: Bantam, 1995. District Attorney Bugliosi prosecuted Charles Manson for the Tate-LaBianca murders, and his book on the case offers many details about Lynette "Squeaky" Fromme.

James C. Clark, *The Murder of James A. Garfield.* Jefferson, NC: McFarland, 1993. This book discusses the life of Charles Guiteau and the murder of President James Garfield.

James W. Clark, *American Assassins: The Darker Side of Politics.* Princeton, NJ: Princeton University Press, 1982. This book offers biographical information about American assassins and discusses their impact on the U.S. government.

Dallas Morning News, *November 22: The Day Remembered as Reported by the Dallas Morning News.* Dallas: Taylor, 1990. Presented by the *Dallas Morning News,* which covered the story of President John F. Kennedy's assassination, this book is an account of that day's events and includes many news photographs.

Justus D. Doenecke, *The Presidencies of James A. Garfield and Chester A. Arthur.* Lawrence: Regents Press of Kansas, 1981. This book provides details regarding the presidency of James Garfield, who was assassinated by Charles Guiteau.

John Douglas and Mark Olshaker, *The Anatomy of Motive.* New York: Lisa Drew Book/Scribners, 1999. A former FBI criminal profiler, Douglas discusses motivations for murder, including assassination.

Albert Ellis and John M. Gullo, *Murder and Assassination.* New York: Lyle Stuart, 1971. Ellis and Gullo have studied the assassin personality in depth and offer many insights into the reasons why assassins are driven to kill American presidents.

Gerald R. Ford, *A Time to Heal: The Autobiography of Gerald R. Ford.* New York: Harper & Row and Reader's Digest, 1979. Ford's autobiography mentions his reaction to the assassination attempt by Lynette Fromme.

Jack and Jo Anne Hinckley, *Breaking Points.* Grand Rapids, MI: Chosen Books (Zondervan), 1985. Written by the parents of John Hinckley Jr., this book offers insights into why Hinckley tried to kill President Ronald Reagan and includes the text of many of his letters.

Margaret Leech, *In the Days of McKinley.* New York: Harper & Brothers, 1959. This book discusses the McKinley presidency at length and includes information about his assassination.

Charles Manson, as told to Nuel Emmons, *Manson in His Own Words.* New York: Grove, 1986. Manson's autobiographical work talks about Lynette Fromme's role in the aftermath of the Tate-LaBianca murders.

James McKinley, *Assassination in America.* New York: Harper & Row, 1977. This book offers an in-depth discussion of American assassinations, although it is most concerned with Lee Harvey Oswald's assassination of President John F. Kennedy.

Thomas C. Reeves, *Gentleman Boss: The Life of Chester Alan Arthur.* New York: Knopf, 1975. This book mentions the aftermath of President James Garfield's assassination.

Charles E. Rosenberg, *The Trial of the Assassin Guiteau: Psychiatry and Law in the Gilded Age.* Chicago: University of Chicago Press, 1968. This book discusses the trial of presidential assassin Charles Guiteau, paying particular attention to questions regarding his sanity.

Eleanor Ruggles, *Prince of Players: Edwin Booth.* New York: W. W. Norton, 1953. This book is an exhaustive biography of actor Edwin Booth but includes information on Edwin's brother, John Wilkes, who assassinated President Abraham Lincoln.

Colin Wilson, *Order of Assassins: The Psychology of Murder.* London: Hart-Davis, 1972. This book discusses the history of assassination and talks about the psychology of the assassin personality.

Periodicals

Mike Feinsilber, "Hinckley, Still 'Dangerous,' Loses Bid for Occasional Freedom," Associated Press, April 15, 1998.

Lance Gay, "Notorious Assassins Cut from Same Disaffected Cloth," Scripts News Service, July 29, 1998.

Mimi Hall, "White House Visit Is No Magic Carpet Ride," *USA Today*, February 5, 1998.

David Hoffman, "Oswald Letter Is Among Documents from Russia," *Washington Post*, June 23, 1999.

Mary Leonard, "The Hinckley Debate: Doctors Say Reagan's Shooter Healthy Enough to Leave Hospital, but Some Wonder if He's Deceiving Them," *Dallas Morning News*, August 7, 1999.

Internet Sources

Liz A. Highleyman, "An Introduction to Anarchism." www.etext.org/Politics/Spunk/library/intro/sp001550.html.

Pan-American Exposition, "Secret Service Guard Ireland Tells Story of Anarchist's Deed." http://intotem.buffnet.net/bhw/panamex/assassination/article5.htm.

INDEX

Grant, Ulysses S., 27, 30, 41–42
Greeley, Horace, 40
Gromyko, Andrei, 64
Guiteau, Charles Julius
    assassinates Garfield, 44–45
    autopsy of, 49
    becomes Christian Perfectionist, 38
    becomes Republican, 41
    childhood of, 37–38
    consequences of act by, 49
    death of, 48–49
    divorce of, 40
    insanity of, 45–46
    insanity plea by, 47–48
    joins Oneida community, 38–39
    marriage of, 40
    opens legal practice, 39–40
    plans assassination, 44
    political motives of, 37, 43–44
    religious speeches by, 40–41
    seeks federal job, 42–43
    sentenced to death, 48
    speaking skills of, 41
    thievery of, 40
    trial of, 47–48
    tries to ruin Blaine's career, 44
    writes book, 41
    writes political speeches, 42

Half-Breeds, 43
Hancock, Winfield Scott, 42
Helter Skelter, 78
heroes, assassins as, 13–15
Herold, David
    becomes coconspirator, 26
    escapes with Booth, 32
    role in conspiracy, 30
    sentenced to hang, 35
    surrender of, 33
Hidell, A., 66, 68, 69
Hinckley, Jack, 87, 92
Hinckley, Jo Anne, 87, 92
Hinckley, John W., Jr.
    arrest of, 95
    becomes hypochondriac, 89
    childhood of, 87
    college years of, 88, 89
    consequences of trial of, 98
    diagnosed with depression, 90
    diagnosed with schizophrenia, 96

engagement of, 97
fights for hospital release, 96–97
flaws in reasoning of, 15
found not guilty, 96
insanity plea by, 95–96
kicked out of home, 92
lies to parents, 88–90, 91
mental instability of, 91–92
mother's protection of, 87
motives for shooting Reagan, 87,
    92–93
obsession with Foster, 91,
    92–93, 96
obsession with *Taxi Driver*,
    90–91
psychiatrist's evaluation of,
    91–92, 96
relies on parents' money, 88–89,
    91, 92
shoots Reagan, 94
stalks Jimmy Carter, 91
suicide attempts by, 95, 96
trial of, 95–96
withdrawn nature of, 87
Hopper, John, 91–92

impatience, of assassins, 16
inadequacy, feelings of, 12–13
insanity defense
    controversy over, 58–60, 98
    in Guiteau's trial, 47–48
    in Hinckley's trial, 95–96
International People's Court of
    Retribution, 82
isolation, of presidents, 17–18

Jackson, Andrew, 8, 10–11
Johnson, Andrew
    assassination attempt on, 30
    political views on South, 15, 35
    possible role in conspiracy, 34

Kennedy, John F.
    assassination of, 66–67
    consequences of killing of, 72–73
    conspiracy theories about, 61
    funeral of, 71
    motives behind killing of, 15
    relations with Castro, 65

PICTURE CREDITS

ABOUT THE AUTHOR

Patricia D. Netzley received her bachelor's degree in English from the University of California at Los Angeles (UCLA). After graduation she worked as an editor at the UCLA Medical Center, where she produced hundreds of medical articles, speeches, and pamphlets.

Netzley became a freelance writer in 1986. She is the author of several books for children and adults, including *The Assassination of President John F. Kennedy* (Macmillan/New Discovery Books, 1994), *Alien Abductions* (Greenhaven Press, 1996), *Issues in the Environment* (Lucent Books, 1998), and the forthcoming *Encyclopedia of Environmental Literature* (ABC-CLIO). Netzley's hobbies are weaving, knitting, and needlework. She and her husband, Raymond, live in Southern California with their three children, Matthew, Sarah, and Jacob.